THRILLS AND
REGRESSIONS

THRILLS AND REGRESSIONS

by

MICHAEL BALINT, M.D.

Consulting Psychiatrist, Tavistock Clinic
Visiting Professor of Psychiatry,
College of Medicine, University of Cincinnati

INTERNATIONAL UNIVERSITIES PRESS, INC.

NEW YORK

ACKNOWLEDGMENTS

I wish to acknowledge the courtesy of the Editors of the *British Journal of Medical Psychology* and of the *International Journal of Psycho-Analysis* for their permission to use in this book material previously published by them.

I am most indebted to Mr. A. S. B. Glover, who once again helped me in editing the manuscript and reading the proofs; the responsibility for the final text, however, is entirely mine. My colleague, Dr. Robert Gosling, kindly undertook again the task of compiling an index.

And finally, I wish to record my thanks to my wife, who not only followed the development of my ideas with helpful criticisms, but contributed to the book Chapter XIV, in which she has described an extension of my ideas which arose out of our many discussions.

London,   M. B.
    January, 1958

CONTENTS

9

CONTENTS

INTRODUCTION

PRIMITIVE attitudes towards the world surrounding us have always been one of the main topics for psycho-analytic research, in both theory and technique. This research has been chiefly concerned with what are called primitive 'object relationships'; only in this phrase 'object' does not refer to objects in the everyday sense but to people, and in the same way object relationship means relationship with people not with objects. This curious usage, which invariably puzzles the uninitiated, is well established among analysts; one speaks of objects of love or hate, of part-objects, one may qualify them as oral, anal, or genital objects, or as internal and external objects, without being troubled in any way by the fact that in reality all this refers to people and not to things. This usage, of course, goes back to Freud, who introduced this technical term in his *Three Essays*.[1] It is important, however, to bear in mind that this happened at the time of the 'physiological bias'[2] in psycho-analysis: the various instincts were then in the focus of interest, the object was thought of as an attribute of the instinct, like its source or aim (see Chapter VII). Since then a good deal has changed in psycho-analytic theory: interest in instincts has steadily decreased, and nowadays objects and object relationships are in the limelight.

This new orientation has brought to light sufficient material to justify my thesis that the development of object relationship and the development of instinctual aims, though they continuously influence each other, are none the less

[1] S. Freud, *Three Essays on Sexuality*. (Standard ed., Vol. VII.) London: Hogarth Press, 1953.
[2] M. Balint, 'Changing Therapeutical Aims and Techniques in Psycho-Analysis' (1949), reprinted in *Primary Love and Psycho-Analytic Technique*. London: Hogarth Press, 1952.

fundamentally different processes.[1] In particular I censured as long ago as 1935 the uncritical use of the adjective 'oral' for the description of everything primitive. This led to a 'distressing and pathetic one-sidedness of our theory. Practically all our technical terms describing the early period of mental life have been derived from objective phenomena and/or subjective experiences of the "oral" sphere; as for instance: greed, incorporation, introjection, internalisation, part-objects; destruction by sucking, chewing, and biting; projection according to the pattern of spitting and vomiting; etc. Sadly enough, we have almost completely neglected to enrich our understanding of these very early, very primitive phenomena by creating theoretical notions and coining technical terms using the experiences, imagery, and implications of other spheres. Such spheres are among others: feeling of warmth, rhythmic noises and movements, subdued nondescript humming, the irresistible and overwhelming effects of tastes and smells, of close bodily contact, of tactile and muscle sensations especially in the hands, and the undeniable power of any and all of these for provoking and allaying anxieties and suspicions, blissful contentment, and dire and desperate loneliness. It is highly probable that because of this omission the time will come when our present theories will be considered as badly deficient and hopelessly lopsided.'[2]

In the first part of this book I wish to discuss a number of observations in the descriptions of which our theoretical considerations suffering under an 'oral' bias fail us. I shall then propose a new approach, and if this proves useful I shall introduce two newly coined technical terms. To round off this part I intend to show that the new ideas and new terms help us considerably in extending our theoretical understanding of a number of common human experiences.

[1] M. Balint, 'Critical Notes on the Theory of the Pregenital Organisations of the Libido' (1935). Reprinted in *Primary Love and Psycho-Analytic Technique.*
[2] M. Balint, *Primary Love and Psycho-Analytic Technique*, p. 156.

INTRODUCTION

The ideas here discussed have been growing in me for a number of years, as a result of which I feel them so much my own that I find it difficult to trace the origin of some of them to a particular author or a particular work. It would be still more difficult for me to disentangle in a fair and just way the stimulations I have received and the contributions I have added. In place of all such detailed and not very important sharing out, I wish to record my great indebtedness to three authors whose work has been most important for the ideas in this book. Sándor Ferenczi, and especially his mostly misunderstood and still not really recognised book *Thalassa*,[1] opened up for me the great possibilities of 'bio-analysis' and suggested the idea of the 'friendly expanses' as the most primitive form of relationship to our environment. Then comes Alice Balint's paper on 'Mother Love and Love for the Mother',[2] one of the most important contributions to our understanding of the mother-child relationship, and her forgotten short paper on 'The Fear of Being Dropped'.[3] Lastly, Imre Hermann, who in several papers[4] called our attention to the crucial role of the hands and of clinging in the development of human relations.

In the second part I shall try to evaluate the usefulness of the new approach for the understanding of some fairly common clinical observations. Our study will be focused on the primitive attitudes towards the world in general, and towards the therapist in particular, as they develop under the impact of the psycho-analytical situation. These phenomena are usually described under the heading of regression. Contrary to established custom, in the course of the discussion less attention will be paid to what might, or does, happen in children than to primitive attitudes easily observable in ordinary everyday adults.

[1] German original, 1924. English translation, New York, *The Psycho-Analytic Quarterly*, 1937.
[2] *Int. J. Psycho-Anal.* (1949), **30**. German original, *I. Z. f. Psa.* (1939), **24**.
[3] *Z. f. psa. Paed.* (1933), **7**.
[4] E.g. *Int. Z. f. Psa.* (1936), **22**; (1941), **26**.

To help my readers to follow my argument through its many ramifications and side issues, I wish to start by stating the main theme in a condensed form. In studying our patients, or indeed man in general, two extreme types emerge. I will quote a concrete instance of each of these types. The first is that of a young student, intelligent, artistic, and well read. She always collected something—books, gramophone records, embroideries, art reproductions, and so on. People meant a great deal to her; she had friends all over the world, white and coloured, young and old, persons of high social position, and simple folk. All of them had to help her in some respect or other, and all were willing to do so, at least for quite a time. This was vitally important to her, as she simply could not live alone. There constantly had to be someone, not necessarily the same person, to whom she could turn for sympathy, understanding, and help, if she came up against a difficulty—and difficulties she had in plenty. It did not matter who the person was—an ambassador of a great power or a penniless coloured student from the Gold Coast, one of our leading literary lights, an O.M., or her professor's young secretary-typist—all had to be there in turn to listen to her, to look after her—and they all did so. Her internal life was in harmony with the outward events; she had always recently received from someone an idea which explained practically everything. Although each such idea gave way in its turn to another, her faithfulness to the idea of the day remained the same. Obviously both people and ideas let her down time and again, but this did not change her, either in her confidence or in her need. She needed objects, both physical and human; she simply could not live without them.

The other patient, also a young woman, a doctor, never wanted to have a home. From her late student days she had gone from one resident post to another, feeling all possessions to be a burden. Finally, as a generous compromise, she agreed with herself to tolerate as many personal belongings as two suitcases could hold. They were suitcases of very moderate size, because one condition of the agreement was that in an emergency she should be able to pick them up by herself and walk away with them. She spoke and read about six languages, and was a voracious reader, but she had to get rid of her books one after another, as they were considered as overweight. She had an uncanny power of winning people's affection, confidence, and deep gratitude; she was really a perfect listener, saying only the right word at the right time. Many people, from royalty to railway porters, from professors of medicine to laboratory stewards, called her their friend and would have done anything for her had she but asked them. Several men asked her to marry them; she always got out of it, but remained the trusted friend of them all for life. Eventually she became a psychiatrist, and mute catatonics, silent for more than a decade, came and sat down with her to talk. She hated artificial feeding for more than one reason, and patients who had to be held down by three or four nurses every evening to be tube fed came with her to the table and ate their meals peacefully, cursing all the other stupid people who, instead of understanding them, used force to no purpose.

Although she did not refuse social invitations, leading in fact a varied and busy social life, she was happiest when left alone, especially if she could feel that, for some days at least, no one would need her to sort out some emotional problem. She adored long walks, but hated it if anyone tried to accompany her. Early in life she had made the discovery that it was a bad bargain to be unkind to people: they would then hate her and never leave her alone. So she developed an admirable skill in dealing with people who needed her, but only so that she might be left at peace afterwards. Objects, both human and physical, were a nuisance to her, though admittedly an interesting and amusing nuisance and an ever-new challenge to her skill to which she never failed to respond. She accepted her successes with some pride and satisfaction, and then got away as painlessly and speedily as possible.

It is true that both these women were ill, indeed very ill. To understand and to describe the difference between them we should need many words and several phrases. And even then the difference, instead of being clearly worked out, would somehow be, as it were, explained away. Very probably, instead of giving a clear-cut picture, many words would obscure the essence of the difference. This difference will be the main topic of this book, and I shall try to keep it right in the focus of my argument. Should my train of thought prove too tortuous for my readers, this difference may serve as a beacon of orientation.

PART ONE

Thrills

FUNFAIRS¹ AND THRILLS

FUNFAIRS exist all over the world, from Bombay to San Francisco and from Alaska to New Zealand. Being so universal, they must respond to some essential human needs. We may even add, knowing what funfairs are, that the essential human needs they satisfy must stem from rather primitive layers of the mind.

Funfairs mean a break in the daily routine, in the exacting discipline of working life. They bring about an easing-off of the strict rules governing the life of society. In this sense they offer something akin to all other 'holidays'. They have, however, special features which are peculiar to funfairs alone. These are represented partly by the kind of amusements and pleasures they offer, and partly by the way people feel towards these amusements and pleasures and behave when enjoying them.

The traditional pleasures found at funfairs may be classified under several headings. My list is certainly incomplete, but I hope it includes the most important items. (*a*) Food; (*b*) aggressive pleasures, such as throwing or shooting at things, smashing things up, etc.; (*c*) pleasures connected with dizziness, vertigo, impairment or loss of stability, such as swings, roundabouts, switchbacks; (*d*) various shows similar to but more primitive and cruder than those offered in circuses and theatres; (*e*) games of chance, either offered openly as such or slightly camouflaged as games of skill, the chances being usually heavily loaded against the player and the prizes offered hardly worth the stake; (*f*) soothsayers; (*g*) lastly, a comparative new-comer, the slot machine, offer-

¹ In America the same kind of enjoyment is offered in 'Amusement Parks'.

ing either various peepshows or games of chance. In this
chapter I shall discuss at any length only the first three kinds
of these pleasures, in the hope that the results will throw some
light on the other groups as well. The main discussion will be
centred on the pleasures involving giddiness.

The first of these three groups of pleasures is the very
primitive catering. The traditional foods sold at funfairs must
generally have two characteristics—they must be very sweet
and very cheap. Often the types of sweets sold there are
peculiar to funfairs and are sold hardly anywhere else or on
any other occasions; this, however, is not an absolute rule.

The next group comprises the aggressive games, such as
target shooting, testing one's strength, and even purely destructive ones like 'breaking up the happy home', where cheap
china is displayed to be smashed up with wooden balls. The
psychodynamics of these two groups of pleasures can be described up to a point by our existing terminology. They both
represent opportunities for regression, i.e. they offer satisfaction for primitive instincts on a fairly primitive level: the
first group to the oral, and the second to the destructive or
aggressive instincts. Seen from this angle, funfairs are safety
valves for pent-up emotions and instinctual urges which, in
civilised and well-brought-up adults, must remain unsatis-
fied, and which are offered periodical outlets on a primitive
level within safe limits.

So far so good. But there is one essential characteristic of
the second group of pleasures which is not so easy to describe
with our present 'oral' terminology. Not only is the individual
allowed to give free rein to his aggressiveness, but—and this
is equally important—he is rewarded for it, his aggressiveness is accepted and approved of by his environment even
though it is broken up and destroyed in the process. The less
anxiety and inhibition the individual feels, the more aggressive or destructive he can be; the more efficient is his performance, the higher is the prize awarded: for hitting the
bull's-eye, for sending the marker to the highest point, for

smashing the most china, and so on. Expressed in psychological terms, this means that the environment not only tolerates aggressiveness and destructiveness and offers opportunities for them, but also, in a way, rejoices with the individual in its own destruction.

This is rather a strange object relationship. Usually one's environment does not go so far; in fact, this is almost an exact reversal of the common situations hitherto studied. In them it is the environment—or one or more powerful persons in it—that is aggressive to the individual. Since the inequality between the individual and his aggressive objects is felt to be overwhelming, any struggle is considered as futile and hopeless, and the conflict is solved by an *identification with the aggressor* leading to a more or less complete submission to his superior powers. The customary theoretical description is: introjection of the aggressive and powerful objects, or splitting off parts of the introjected objects as the internal persecutors, and so on. In quite simple language this means that ever after we seem to help bring about our own humiliation, to work for a victory of our adversaries, perhaps even to the extent of enjoying the strains and pains caused by our own frustration and misery; that is, by *their* satisfaction. In funfairs apparently this state of affairs is turned into the opposite. *We* are allowed to be aggressive and destructive; the environment does not show any resistance; in fact, offers itself as a willing target; moreover, it definitely rewards us the more highly the more destructive we are able to be.

To describe this hitherto unstudied object relationship with our present terminology would be anything but easy, though not impossible; for instance, by straining a point and using the idea of projective identification. This would explain why the individual should *feel* that his environment agrees with, and even rewards, his aggressiveness directed against it; but it would not help us to understand the fact that the environment really *does* so, and still less why this queer object relationship is mutually satisfactory both to the individual and his environment.[1] On the other hand, if we use my idea of primary love the theoretical description of this object relationship causes no difficulty. Primary love is a relationship in which only one partner may have demands and claims; the other partner (or partners, i.e. the whole world) must have no interests, no wishes, no demands, of his or her own. There is, and must be, a complete harmony, i.e. a complete identity of wishes and satisfactions. The English saying, 'What's sauce for the goose is sauce for the gander', is here literally and absolutely true; the environment must be in complete harmony with the demands and enjoyments of the individual. The rejoicing of the environment on being destroyed by the individual, to the extent of offering rewards for its own destruction—as happens in funfairs—is one more fairly strong argument for the theory of primary love. Looking at it from this angle, funfairs offer possibilities of limited regression to this early phase of human relationship.

However, it must be added that there are important differences among individuals in the extent to which they are able to regress towards enjoying these kinds of pleasures. Some revel in these possibilities, get excited, slightly mad, while others are not interested, are even bored or disgusted. There are also others who timidly try but are inhibited and can never be any good at it, and still others who are contemptuous, apprehensive, or even frightened. Later we shall have to go into the dynamics of these various attitudes in more detail.

Still greater theoretical difficulties are encountered when we try to describe the amusements of the third group, which include the traditional swings, roundabouts, switchbacks, and their more and more complicated and ingenious modern

[1] The condition that the environment, although damaged or even destroyed, is satisfied, differentiates this primitive relationship from another group of cases in which destructiveness is also rewarded, as, e.g., in the case of bravery in war. There at least one part of the environment—the enemy—is not pleased at all and tries hard to defend itself.

22

forms. All the amusements in this group are connected with giddiness and vertigo; that is to say, with a situation in which a particular form of anxiety is aroused and borne. The form of this anxiety can be described as loss of balance, of stability, of the firm contact with the safe earth, and so on. Some people react instinctively, almost reflex-like, to this kind of anxiety by clutching at something firm, or, in still greater anxiety, by pressing their whole body against a firm and safe object. While normally the planting of the feet firmly on the ground gives them enough security, in 'giddy' situations this does not seem to be sufficient.

In all amusements and pleasures of this kind three characteristic attitudes are observable: (*a*) some amount of conscious fear, or at least an awareness of real external danger; (*b*) a voluntary and intentional exposing of oneself to this external danger and to the fear aroused by it; (*c*) while having the more or less confident hope that the fear can be tolerated and mastered, the danger will pass, and that one will be able to return unharmed to safety. This mixture of fear, pleasure, and confident hope in face of an external danger is what constitutes the fundamental elements of all *thrills*.

Let us briefly examine in what way other thrills resemble those offered in funfairs. Some are connected with *high speed*, as in all kinds of racing, horse-riding and jumping, motor racing, skating, ski-ing, tobogganing, sailing, flying, etc. Others are connected with *exposed situations*, like various forms of jumping and diving, rock climbing, gliding, taming wild animals, travelling into unknown lands, etc. Lastly, there is a group of thrills which are connected with *unfamiliar* or even *completely new forms of satisfaction*, either in the form of a new object or of an unfamiliar method of pleasure. The obvious new object is a virgin, and it is amazing how many thrills claim this adjective. One speaks of virgin land, a virgin peak, or a virginal route to a peak, virgin realms of speed, and so on. On the whole, any new sexual partner is a thrill, especially if he or she belongs to another race, colour, or creed. The new forms of pleasure include among others: new food, new clothes, new customs, up to new forms of 'perverse' sexual activities. In all these phenomena we find the same three fundamental factors described above: the objective external danger giving rise to fear, the voluntary and intentional exposure of oneself to it, and the confident hope that all will turn out well in the end.

Another group of thrills, much more primitive and general but equally important, is made up of some forms of children's games. The majority of them are based on our three fundamental factors. A typical example may suffice: Tom Tiddler's Ground. It is highly significant that in practically all games of this kind the security is called either 'house' or 'home'. This holds good not only for English but for all the languages known to me. All these games consist (*a*) of an external danger, represented by the catcher, the seeker, the chaser, and (*b*) of the other players leaving the zone of security, the 'home', accepting exposure to danger more or less voluntarily, (*c*) in the confident hope that somehow or other they will reach security again. There are innumerable games of this kind, like blind man's buff, hide and seek, tig, rounders, musical chairs, oranges and lemons, to quote a few, and not forgetting cricket, where on the whole runs may be scored only by leaving the safe zone.

Lastly, we have the professionals, who are paid for their skill which causes thrills to the spectators and possibly also to themselves. They are called *acrobats*, and are a very old and venerable profession, represented already on classical Greek vases and possibly even on frescoes found at Knossos and dating back to 1600 B.C. Their performances include amazingly varied forms, some of them of great antiquity, seen and admired already in the Roman circuses, among them tightrope walkers (*funambuli*), bareback riders (*desultores*), tumblers, jugglers, and possibly also contortionists. In more modern times they have mastered the fixed and the flying trapeze, the unsupported ladder, and so on. The thrills caused in the spectators increase with the distance of the acrobat from the safe earth and the precariousness of his attachment to some firm structure—which in the last analysis means also the earth. We shall have to return presently to this observation.

The psychology of these thrills has not been studied to any extent, and it is no wonder therefore that our terminology, based mainly on early 'oral' experiences, fails rather sadly when we attempt to describe these phenomena. In order to be able to discuss them I propose to coin two new terms. Greek scholars among my readers will know that 'acrobat' means literally 'he who walks on his toes', i.e. away from the safe earth. Taking this word as my model, I have coined 'philobat' to describe one who enjoys such thrills; from which one can easily form the adjective 'philobatic' to describe the pleasures and activities, and the abstract noun 'philobatism' to describe the whole field. We need another term to describe the apparent opposite of a philobat, one who cannot stand swings and switchbacks, who prefers to clutch at something firm when his security is in danger. For this I propose 'ocnophil', derived from the Greek verb ὀκνέω, meaning 'to shrink, to hesitate, to cling, to hang back'. From this word we get the adjective 'ocnophilic' and the abstract noun 'ocnophilia'.[1]

[1] I wish to express my gratitude to David Eichholz, Reader in Classics at the University of Bristol, who, greatly amused by my efforts to find suitable words for my ideas, helped me to devise these two terms.

II

PHILOBATISM AND OCNOPHILIA

THE introduction of new words calls for justification; their usefulness has to be proved. I propose to do this in two ways. I intend to show, first, that by using these two terms we can discuss certain human experiences more easily than without them; and, secondly, that in this way we can better understand these experiences and their dynamism. Let us therefore briefly survey what we already know about thrills; that is, philobatism and ocnophilia. This will help us at the same time to clear our way for the next step, since this survey will bring us to the point which our theory of these phenomena has reached.

Let us start with the children's games. As I have said, the zone of security is always called either 'home' or 'house', which points to its being a symbol for the safe mother. We have seen also that all thrills entail the *leaving* and *rejoining* of security. The pleasures experienced in either of these two phases—that is, either when staying in security or when leaving it in order to return to it—are very primitive, self-evident, and apparently in no need of explanation—although it must be stated that not every adult can enjoy them equally. True, some adults seem to be at ease only when in the state of stable security; others, on the contrary, enjoy leaving it in search of adventures and thrills and show signs of boredom and irritation if they have to forgo them for any length of time. Somehow, however, correctly or incorrectly, one gets the impression that ocnophilia might be the older and more primitive of the two attitudes. Later we shall have to examine more closely how far this impression is misleading.

One's relation to security—that is to say, one's behaviour in the state of security—appears *prima facie* to be simple, uncomplicated, practically unstructured, whereas one's relation to the intervening state, while enjoying the thrill, seems very complicated and involved indeed. A readily available parallel is the way the infant clings to his mother before leaving her, before walking away. This is undoubtedly true, but it should not be forgotten that this difference might be caused merely by the unequal rate of maturation of the various systems of motility and not necessarily by those of the mind; that is to say, because the nerve centres and musculature of the mouth and arms involved in clinging mature earlier than those concerned with walking and maintaining equilibrium. It would be wise to be cautious in our inference from these observations about the existence of certain mental attitudes; as, for instance, taking the nipple and sucking it appears in a full-time baby at about the same time as pushing the nipple out of the mouth and turning the head away. It is even possible that the pushing out might be the earlier function, as premature babies often have to be taught to take the nipple, although they can already swallow faultlessly. What we can say at this moment is that the relative chronology of philobatism and ocnophilia is uncertain, although it is certain that they are both very primitive. We shall return to the problem of chronology in Chapter IX.

Nevertheless, ocnophilia impresses us as the more spontaneous, almost reflex-like attitude, whereas one cannot state with certainty where philobatism really belongs. In addition the appearance of ocnophilic tendencies in seemingly purely philobatic situations suggests a kind of regressive trend and, conversely, a more primitive nature on the part of ocnophilia. To quote a few examples: the tight-rope walker holds a pole in his hands, the lion tamer a whip, the conductor of an orchestra a baton, and so on. Moreover, the car driver has to learn not to grip the wheel and the skier not to press his sticks; similarly a boxer, a weight-lifter, an oarsman, in fact every athlete, has to be taught not to tense up his neck and jaw muscles when making a supreme effort. As already mentioned, the performance of an acrobat is valued more highly if he does *not* use his hands; if he hangs from the trapeze by his feet or his teeth, lets go the handlebars of the bicycle, drops the reins of his horse when standing on its back, enters the lion's cage without a whip, or, to come down to the level of ordinary human beings, rides on the round-abouts standing up, without leaning on or holding on to any-thing. A traditional trick, often used by acrobats, which always increases the excitement, the thrill, is to get rid of and throw away parts of their equipment in an already exposed situation or before entering into a still more exposed one. We may even add that the transitional objects of young children and toddlers described recently by Winnicott[1] are nearly always clutched, pressed, or cuddled; furthermore, all artists must have something in their hands: a brush, a chisel and mallet, a baton, a bow, a drawing pencil and ruler, a pen, and so on. In general, even statues tend to hold something fast, no matter whether they represent soldiers, scientists, artists, politicians, or martyrs, and even the Virgin and the Infant Jesus apparently must have something in their hands. So it seems that to hold on to something, to have something in one's hand, is more primitive and more general than being independent, being completely on one's own, with hands empty. The things that we cling to—the ocno-philic objects—appear in the first instance to be symbols of security; that is, the safe, loving mother.

After this digression, let us turn to the behaviour in the philobatic state. The first feature that impresses itself upon us is that the individual is on his own, away from every sup-port, relying on his own resources. The outward expression of this attitude is a brave, erect stance; crawling on all fours, as we all know, is not an heroic posture; whereas walking, and especially stalking and strutting, usually is. In this respect it should not be forgotten that walking in an erect position

---

[1] D. W. Winnicott, 'Transitional Objects and Transitional Pheno-mena', *Int. J. Psycho-Anal.*, **34** (1953), 89.

means being fairly well away from the safe earth, the only contact with it being through the soles of the feet. We understand now why the thrill is the greater the farther we dare get away from safety—in distance, in speed, or in exposure; that is to say, the more we can prove our independence. A further relevant factor is the duration of this independent state, the length of time we can hold out in it. This explains why it is so attractive for some people to undertake crossings of the oceans in small boats, in one-man dinghies, or on rafts, as in the famous Kon-Tiki expedition, or to remain in the air in a glider for hours or even longer than a day.

These observations suggest that philobatism is symbolically related to erection and potency, although it is difficult to decide whether philobatism should be considered as an early, primitive stage of genitality or, the other way round, as a retrospective, secondary genitalisation in adult age of an originally non-genital function. In any case, this inter-relation explains the other aspect of the objects the philobat clings to, which we called ocnophilic objects. The whip of the lion-tamer, the pole of the tight-rope walker, the sticks of the skier, the baton of the conductor, the sword or rifle of the soldier, the artist's tools, the pilot's joy-stick, are undoubtedly symbols of the erect, potent penis. Having an ocnophilic object with us means also being in possession of a powerful, never-flagging penis, magically reinforcing our own potency, our own confidence. From this we can understand the special affection people have for their particular ocnophilic objects. The skier must have his own particular sticks, the lion-tamer his favourite whip, the tennis player his special racket, the cricketer his favourite bat, the conductor his baton, the artist his brush, and so on. Possessing these well-proved ocnophilic objects, he feels himself in possession of almost magic powers, and is much more confident in braving the hazards of the philobatic state.

Seen from this angle, we may say that the philobatic thrills represent in a way the primal scene in symbolic form. A powerful and highly skilled man produces on his own a powerful erection, lifting him far away from security, performing in his lofty state incredible feats of valour and daring, after which, in spite of untold dangers, he returns unhurt to the safe mother earth. In this connection the earth has a double aspect corresponding to the ambivalent situation; she is dangerous because of her irresistible attraction which, if unconditionally surrendered to, may cause mortal damage; but at the same time she is loving and forgiving, offering her embracing safety to the defiant hero on his skilful return. It is traditional in the circus for the hero-acrobat while performing high up in the air to be assisted, admired, and finally received back to the ground by an attractive young girl. Acrobatics, therefore, are one special form of shows all of which symbolically represent the primal scene. I mentioned in Chapter I that funfairs offer also primitive shows of various kinds. One type of showpiece is either beautiful, attractive women, or frightening, odd, and strange females; the other type is powerful, boasting, challenging men. Simplified to the bare essentials, practically all stage plays or novels, however highbrow, are still concerned with these three kinds of human ingredients.

The specific difference between shows in general and philobatic shows and feats is the presence of *real external danger*. In classical times the real danger was, in fact, naked cruel death and not merely a threatening possibility of it. People were killed in reality by wild beasts, in gladiator fights, mock battles, and so on. As civilisation progressed, this real death was replaced gradually by illusions, as in the theatre (the last scene of *Hamlet* ends with about *half a dozen corpses* on the stage), or by the threatening presence of real danger of death as in the modern circus. However, both in the circus and in the theatre the performers are professionals who have inherited from the ancient heroes all the highly powered and ambivalent emotional tributes of the general public, such as awe, envy, contempt, admiration, and so on.

The dynamic reason for this ambivalent respect is that acrobats and actors are allowed and dare to perform publicly philobatic acts symbolising primal scenes. The community, however, is allowed to participate in the form of passive spectators only, thrilled by identification.

The question of what happened, mainly during the nineteenth century, that turned the spectators into actors is an interesting problem and worth a proper study. It is possible that this change is only one symptom of a general tendency of that epoch, perhaps best expressed by Nietzsche, 'to live dangerously'. As I wish to continue with our main topic, the few data that I can contribute to this study will be discussed in Chapter XIII.

We have to turn now to the question why some people expose themselves unnecessarily to real dangers in search of thrills, while others cannot even bear the thought of exposing themselves to dangers, or in other words: What are the relevant mechanisms involved in these two—apparently equally irrational—attitudes?

III

OBJECT RELATIONSHIPS AND ANXIETIES

As a preliminary step, I wish to use for discussion rather extreme forms both of ocnophilia and philobatism, which of course are rare. In fact, these extreme cases are hardly ever met with in reality; what we are commonly confronted with are varied mixtures of the two object relationships to be described; where one attitude may be used to repress or even over-compensate the other in various combinations in the various layers of the mind.

First let us take *ocnophilia*, where some object relationship is unconditional and the involvement of fear obvious. This state of affairs is admirably expressed by the Greek word ὀκνέω chosen to describe this attitude. Its meaning is 'to cling to', 'to shrink', 'to hesitate', 'to hang back', with the implicit meaning that this happens because of fear, shame, or pity in relation to an object. Obviously there must be an object available, otherwise the individual cannot cling. Accordingly the ocnophilic world consists of objects, separated by horrid empty spaces. The ocnophil lives from object to object, cutting his sojourns in the empty spaces as short as possible. Fear is provoked by leaving the objects, and allayed by rejoining them.

The actual relation to the objects is very primitive. Quite often we find obvious signs that the relation does not go farther than the part that is clung to, i.e. it does not necessarily include the whole object. 'A drowning man will clutch at a straw' admirably describes this attitude, and it is well worth noting that this proverb is truly international. The reaction of an ocnophilic man in the face of fear shows perhaps most clearly the persistence of part objects in an adult.

As in every case of really primitive object relationship, there are to be found in the relationships to ocnophilic objects all the features described as characteristic of primary love. The demand for the object is absolute. If the need is felt, the object must needs be there; moreover, in the state of need, no regard, consideration, or concern can be paid to the object, it is simply taken for granted. In other words, this means that the relation to an ocnophilic object is definitely predepressive.

The *ocnophilic clinging* to objects or part objects is the best-studied object relationship in psycho-analysis. Perhaps its most important quality is that, always and unavoidably, it gets frustrated. Apart from the fact that the object clung to is —in adult life—always a mere substitute, never permitting full satisfaction, there are several features inherent in the ocnophilic object relationship which make frustration inevitable. First, the object, however kindly attuned to the subject, has nevertheless its own life, and must occasionally go its own way, which conversely means that there is a constant danger of the individual being dropped by his object, which danger periodically becomes a bitter fact. If a part-object is used for clinging, which quite frequently happens, the relationship can never be fully satisfactory for the ocnophil. The part object, more often in the individual's fantasy but occasionally also in reality, may be detached from the whole object, causing all sorts of complications such as that the whole object is now damaged, is of much less value, and, most important, that the detached part—i.e. the part remaining available to the ocnophil—is of *no use* whatever. There are innumerable comic and tragic scenes in plays, novels, and in real life in which someone clings desperately to something felt to be very precious, saves it at great risk to himself from all sorts of perils, and then, finally arriving in safety, examines it at close quarters, and discovers that the precious object is really *no good* at all. Lastly, the real aim can never be achieved by clinging. The real aim is to be held by the object and not to cling desperately to it; this being held should happen without even the need to express any wish for it. It is the most cherished aim of every one of us that our environment should meet our wishes—especially our wish for security—without us even asking for it. To ask for security and still more to use force to move our object to grant us security—i.e. to cling to it—is always humiliating and inherently only a very poor second best. This kind of relationship cannot but lead inevitably to ambivalence.

The whole world is different for the *philobat*. Provided the elements are not too inclement—e.g. no storm or gale is raging—the pilot is safe in the skies, the sailor on the high seas, the skier on the slopes, the driver on the open road, the parachutist in the air. Danger and fear are evoked only if an object appears that has to be negotiated; the pilot has to take off or land, the sailor to enter or leave harbour, the skier to negotiate rocks, trees, or crevasses, the driver to mind other cars or pedestrians on the road, the parachutist to jump off or to land. We may therefore say that the philobatic world consists of friendly expanses dotted more or less densely with dangerous and unpredictable objects. One lives in the friendly expanses, carefully avoiding hazardous contacts with potentially dangerous objects. Whereas the ocnophilic world is structured by physical proximity and touch, the philobatic world is structured by safe distance and sight. An easy proof of how closely philobatism is connected with sight and ocnophilia with touch may be found if one tries to move about blindfolded in an unfamiliar environment. When losing orientation by sight one really lives from object to object, feels safe as long as one is in touch with them, and rather uncertain when one is alone in the empty spaces between them. It must be stressed, however, that it is not the empty spaces themselves that are felt as dangerous. The real danger remains the same as we have met in any of the philobatic situations: the sudden emergence of a hazardous object that has to be negotiated.

Whereas the ocnophil lives in the illusion that as long as he is in touch with a safe object he is himself safe, the philobat's illusion is that apart from *his* own proper equipment he needs no objects, certainly no one particular object. The ocnophil is confident that *his chosen object will 'click in'* with him and protect him against the empty, unfamiliar, and possibly dangerous world; the philobat feels that using his equipment he can certainly cope with any situation; *the world as a whole will 'click in'* and he will be able to avoid treacherous objects. While the ocnophil has to presume that he can win the favour and partiality of his object, the philobat feels that it is within his power to conquer the 'world' without relying on the favours of untrustworthy individual objects. On this point he is perhaps unduly optimistic, confident, and trusting, both with regard to the clemency of the elements and the extent of his own skill. His optimism is only limited by his need, an almost compelling need, to watch the world around him; a need, it is true, leading to a great variety of pleasures. As already mentioned, the philobatic world is structured by safe distance and sight. This need to watch is a true counterpart of the ocnophil's compelling need to touch. However, there is a danger of the need to watch developing into a paranoid attitude; but this danger is equally present in the ocnophil's compelling need for close contact.

What is it that the philobat has to watch? He watches for objects appearing from somewhere or nowhere, objects that are whole objects, and are felt either as ugly, indifferent, uncaring, occasionally even hostile, disturbing the harmony of the friendly expanses around him, or, on the other hand, as beautiful, friendly, caring, and helpful, enhancing the harmony of his friendly expanses. In some way his objects are reminiscent of the secondary characters in fairy tales, who may be either helpers and associates of the hero or his adversaries; and a further characteristic of theirs is that they can be changed suddenly from one class to the other by apparently minor events. In some layers of the mind these secondary characters may symbolise, as the case may be, the magic penis, or breast, or vagina, and so on. For my argument the main point is that they invariably appear as whole objects, presenting a psychological problem to the hero who has, so to speak, to conquer them by solving the problem or puzzle presented. This kind of conquest—changing an indifferent or hostile object into a co-operative partner—is achieved, as are all such conquests, by showing consideration, regard, or concern about them. The standard form is 'Lucky for you that you called me granny' (or uncle, or aunt, and so on), 'or else it would have been the worse for you'. In some fairy tales the concern shown by the hero or heroine amounts to true 'looking after', as in *The Beauty and The Beast*, where the Beast is cured and changed by Beauty's careful psychological nursing.

All these emotional attitudes, described as regard, consideration, concern, and looking after, obviously belong to the post-depressive phase, but in addition they all have close connection with distance and sight. The three synonymous words, 'concern', 'consideration', 'regard', came from the Norman-French into English, and were already well established and widely used in the fifteenth century. It is remarkable that in their original meaning they all describe a state of intense looking at an object from some distance. The same is true of the corresponding words in German (*Rücksicht*) and Hungarian (*tekintet*). In contradistinction to this, another word which describes a similar, but still more considerate, attitude is derived from the ocnophilic world, and that is 'tact'. These two words, 'consideration' and 'tact', give a good idea of the difference between the ocnophilic and philobatic worlds.

The French equivalent of these three synonymous words is rather difficult to find; perhaps *égards* comes nearest to them, in that on the one hand it is made up of *garder*—i.e. 'to guard', 'to watch', 'to look out'—while on the other hand it contains also the preposition 'é' corresponding to the Latin 'ex', denoting distance. In the same way two of the three synonymous English words, 'concern' and 'consideration', contain the preposition 'con', meaning 'taking together', diminishing the distance.

The imagery of the frequently used English expression 'to look after' somebody belongs to the same philobatic world. In a way it tells the whole story of a happy and close proximity ended for good, the object moving away from us, and from now on, if we want to restore a semblance of the old proximity, the only thing we can do is to 'look after' it. The cognate German words *Nachsicht, nachsehen,* are perhaps still more melancholic. They mean 'making allowances', 'forbearing', 'forgiving', without even the promise of restoring the lost proximity at the price of caring or nursing, as the English 'look after' does.

So it seems that these philobatic attitudes are all connected with the acceptance of separation from the object and with looking at it from a distance, however small. Obviously they can develop only after an emotional acceptance of the fact that subject and object have separate existences, that both must, and do, continue to exist even when they are no longer in close contact with each other; in other words, after accepting that life and some kindness are possible even for one separated from his love object either temporarily or even for good. Only after this fact has been emotionally accepted is one able to allow the love object to go on its way and to have 'regard' for it, to 'con-sider' it or be 'con-cerned' about it, or even to 'look after' it.

As mentioned, for the philobat the world is structured by safe distance and sight, and for the ocnophil by physical proximity and touch. In the event of fear or anxiety, the reaction of the ocnophil is to get as near as possible to his object, to squat or sit down, go on all fours, lean towards, or even press his whole body to the protecting object. Parallel with this he turns his face away, even shuts his eyes, trying not to see the danger. All this is markedly present in any of the so-called giddy situations, like looking down from excessive heights into depths and precipices. Every rock-climber knows these reactions and the real dangers connected with them, especially that of not being able to look round properly and, instead of making use of proper grips and footholds, trying to press the whole body unnecessarily to the rockface.

The reaction of the philobat is what is generally called the heroic one: turning towards the approaching danger, facing it in order to watch it, keeping away from objects that offer false security, standing upright on his own. The condemned man is usually blindfolded, taking for granted an ocnophilic reaction in the face of mortal danger. In the same way it is generally regarded as heroic when the philobat asks to face the firing squad erect and with open eyes, although this is just as much according to his nature as the ocnophil's wish not to see the danger and to be allowed to lean on something.

I mentioned in the beginning of this chapter that the examples described are extremes. Just as no one is an absolute sadist or masochist, so no one is an absolute philobat or ocnophil; but in the same way as certain people show definite sadistic propensities in certain spheres of their mental life, while others in the same spheres are mainly masochistic, the same holds true of the philobatic and ocnophilic attitudes. Thus, for example, with regard to the sphere of thought, in practically every language we find characteristic phrases borrowed from these experiences. In English we say that someone has a sticky mind, his thinking is bogged down, he clings to words, phrases, habits, or ideas; he cannot let go or drop a habit, or his ways of thinking, pastime, or occupation; another has free flight of ideas, flits from one thing to another, is a lone wolf, etc. It is surprising how many of our words denoting understanding of a problem, a human being, or a situation, are derived either from ocnophilic or from philobatic imagery. 'Understand', *verstehen*, are obviously connected with standing. The corresponding Hungarian word *megért* literally means 'finally arriving at'. On the other hand, *comprehend*, *comprendre*, *grasp*, *grip*, the German *begreiffen*, *Begriff*, *zusammenfassen*, derive from ocnophilia. From the philobatic world we get the words 'explain', 'explicit', the French *expliquer*, meaning to make things plain; that is, to restore the harmony of the friendly expanses by removing from it every disturbing object. I am quite certain that the same will be true of practically every language.

These phrases, among others, show that the philobatic and ocnophilic attitudes are not confined to the external physical world, to our relationship with people, but apply similarly to our internal experiences, to our relationship to ideas and ideals. We know that there are people who can feel safe and secure only if they are in close contact with an object or objects, i.e. familiar people, ideas, and beliefs. These people cannot bear it if they are *out of touch* with their familiar world of objects, ideas, beliefs, conventions, and if they should suddenly be confronted with a new idea, a new form of experience, or some uncertain physical or emotional situation, they feel disconcerted and will long to return to the safety of their accustomed ways of thinking, feeling, and being. They feel lost without their objects, external or internal, and so they can criticise or exchange them only with difficulty and diffidence. Their objects must be preserved at all costs, since life without them would be unbearable, chaotic. Justifiably or not, the ocnophil feels that he *is* safe with them, is protected by them; in fact, they must be there for him, it simply cannot be otherwise.[1] Moreover,

---

[1] When looking for a term to describe the ocnophilic world, Mr. Eichholz proposed 'sosichrematic'. It is most instructive to examine the cluster of associations surrounding this proposed term; it seems to show that the Greek language, for one, knew a good deal about the psychological implications of ocnophilia. The first part of this word, σώσω, means (a) to keep alive, to save from death, and in the passive form, to be helped, to recover from illness, to escape, to be saved; (b) (with regard to material things) to keep safe, to preserve. The second part is still more interesting. 'χρῆμα' means (a) urge, need, and then the thing that one needs or uses; (b) material goods, wealth and property;

these people do not seem to be able to trust their world of objects to look after them; as they feel that their objects cannot be relied upon to be there for them, they must cling; the only way for them to feel secure is to be 'in constant touch' with their important objects, people, ideas, etc. Objects are merely accepted but not trusted; they are needed but cannot be let out of control. In the next chapters we shall examine the question of what the real nature of this relationship is and, in particular, whether it can be called love or hate.

Contrariwise, the philobat is apparently independent, confident, and self-contained. He feels that he can avoid or find objects, external or internal, as he chooses; in fact, he is never in doubt that he can find new objects, new ideas, and he even enjoys dropping the old and finding the new. In a way it is only his freedom that matters, and seemingly he does not care much whether he is loved or not, as he is certain that if need be he can make any object love him.

These people apparently are all out to preserve the feeling of safety in the harmonious mix-up with their friendly expanses, even after the emergence of objects into their world. They seem to wish to avoid independent objects, and may indeed be found to cherish only those objects over which they feel they have complete and absolute control, which are really part of themselves—the kind that a sportsman will call his gear or equipment. These people can have objects (which term again includes ideas, people, etc.) which they may leave and rejoin at their whim without any fear that this might lead to recrimination or resentment; in fact, it is doubtful

(c) business matter, transaction, affair. The plural of the same word means objects or things in general, or a great deal, a lot. From the same root is derived 'χράομαι' meaning (a) to desire, need, yearn for, be in need of, to be lacking in; (b) to experience, to suffer, to be subject to. Another form of the same word, 'χρήμω', means to desire, to long, to crave for. The root itself, 'χρή', is a defective verb, used only in the third person singular, denoting the absolute necessity of some action, like the English colloquialism 'he must *needs* do it'. 'Sosichrematic' therefore means someone who must at all costs keep safe and preserve the objects that gratify his imperative needs.

whether these objects—the equipment—are felt to have any freedom of their own. This leads us to the same problem as with the ocnophil, i.e. what the true nature of this relationship is, and whether it should be considered love or hate.

Admittedly the two types described consist of extremes. One would like to think of an ideal person who, while not abandoning his wish to achieve the one-ness and harmony of his early experience, can still accept objects as friendly and yet independent, who need not deny them their freedom either by clinging or by degrading them to the rank of 'equipment'.

Before embarking on the next stage of our journey, let us survey our itinerary hitherto as we see it from our present standpoint. We started at the funfairs, where we found an intriguing harmony and co-operation between the environment and the individual, a harmony and co-operation which remained undisturbed even while the individual destroyed his environment. Of all psycho-analytic theories the theory of primary love is the only one that can explain this common observation. Our real journey, however, started with the study of the class of pleasures connected with giddiness. We found that some children's games, acrobatics, and thrills in general showed structures similar in many respects to those of the giddy pleasures in funfairs. We found, further, that these pleasures were too difficult to describe and still more difficult to explain on the basis of our existing theories. Two new words, ocnophilia and philobatism, were then proposed, and with their help we were able to describe fairly satisfactorily all the phenomena mentioned. The chief result of this study is that both ocnophilia and philobatism are primitive attitudes, but their exact chronological place in mental development is as yet uncertain. This uncertainty was to be expected, since up to this point our study has been confined to adults only. Before leaving the world of adults, I propose to examine in the next three chapters the connections between these new ideas and some fundamental psycho-analytic concepts.

IV

AGGRESSIVITY AND AUTO-EROTISM

THE popular words used to describe the various giddy amusements and pleasures in funfairs will offer us a good starting-point. 'Swing' is an old Teutonic word, whose original meaning was 'to swing a weapon', later any other contrivance, and still later, in the intransitive sense, 'to swing on a rope'. This evolution was achieved fairly early, as by about 1500 'swing' already meant, in the colloquial sense, to hang or to be hanged. 'Switch' is a cognate word with 'swish'; its original meaning was to brandish a weapon causing a high-pitched noise, from which there developed the intransitive sense of being brandished. 'Thrill', cognate with 'thirl', meant to pierce, to penetrate, to bore something, again causing a high-pitched sound. Corresponding to these highly aggressive meanings, philobatic people are usually imagined as robust, upstanding, conquering heroes, enjoying their independence, unflinchingly facing dangers, and defiantly going their own way.

This element of aggressiveness is undoubtedly present in all philobatic activities. Still it remains problematic how this aggressiveness towards objects described by transitive verbs turned into the activity described by intransitive verbs. In other words, how the active voice turned, not into the passive but the middle voice: 'I swing (something)' became not 'I am swung' but 'I swing myself', i.e. 'I swing'. The state described by this middle voice, or intransitive form, is reminiscent of primary love previously mentioned. There is no clash between the subject and his object; on the contrary, there is complete harmony. 'I swing myself'= 'My primary object swings me' = 'I swing'. One would be equally justified in stating either that there is *no* aggressiveness in this action or that the aggressiveness has been turned *outward* towards the world, or that the aggressiveness has been turned *inward* towards the self. All three mutually exclusive descriptions are equally true, as ought to be the case with a primitive undifferentiated relationship. That all three statements about this primitive form of aggressiveness are equally true is usually overlooked by certain theoreticians of psycho-analysis. Contentedly they point out that one or the other of these statements is true for describing a primitive state, and use this part-truth as a convincing argument for their particular thesis. Neglecting the fact that all three descriptions are simultaneously and equally true permits them to pass over the important phase of primary love, which alone can explain this simultaneity and equivalence.

Remarkably, the situation is utterly different with regard to thrill, which can be used only either in the passive form 'I am thrilled', or in the active 'it is thrilling', 'she thrills me', both of which presuppose an external object and an established relationship between object and subject. I cannot offer any explanation for this difference except perhaps the fact that 'thrill', in the sense of highly exciting pleasure, is a fairly new word, dating back only to the late nineteenth century. Moreover, as far as I know, it is an exclusively English word; no other language has its equivalent.

The same grammatical forms—middle voice, reflexive or intransitive forms—are also used for the expression of another most important relationship, the field of auto-erotic activities, from scratching to masturbation. In this field also, according to grammar, there is no object or, psychologically more correctly, subject and object are identical.

It would be most important for our understanding of auto-erotic activities if we could decide whether this identity of subject and object (or the lack of external objects) is the result of a progression or of a regression. Perhaps the problem is incorrectly formulated when stated in this way, and the real question which should be asked is how much of the auto-erotic activities is due to progression and how much to regression. It has long been known that over-indulgently brought up children masturbate on the whole much more intensely than the average child. On the other hand, if the environment is greatly indifferent right from the start and the neglected child hardly ever experiences loving human contact, both his object relationships and his auto-erotic activities will become stunted, as was clearly demonstrated by R. Spitz's films on severely deprived children. It seems therefore that satisfactory object relationships and satisfactory auto-erotism are parallel lines of development having possibly the same source. If we can discover this common source and study its attributes and potentialities, we may be able to answer the question—what in auto-erotism is due to regression and what to progression? In my opinion the common origin will prove to be, what I called, primary love.

One more digression awaits us before I can return to my main theme. Auto-erotic activities, in fact all sexual activities as well as thrills, have a good deal in common. Their basic pattern is the same three-act drama: a relatively safe and quiet initial state, an intentional raising of the tension, in the confident hope that in the end everything will turn out well. Genital activity, however, leads to orgasm, and in this way differs from all other sexual pleasures and thrills, which hardly ever reach that intensity. Although in their deeper layer philobatic thrills symbolically represent the primal scene, phenomenologically they are much nearer to auto-erotism. Philobatic heroism is, in a way, phallic-narcissistic heroism, most manly and at the same time very childish, never fully mature. This is the reason why it has always to be boosted up somewhat, even a good deal. In other words, it is a difficult task to explain to a sceptic the immanent values of having won the 220 yards hurdles, holding the world record for the high jump, having ascended the highest peak in the world, or made the deepest descent into a cave or the depths of the ocean. This is a sad state of affairs because, in a way, it is equally true of all sublimated activities, including the arts and pure sciences. It seems to be the male's fate that even his highest and purest achievements cannot be fully divested of infantile propensities.

In spite of many warnings, one by Freud himself,[1] not to equate aggressiveness and activity with masculinity on the one hand and masochism and passivity with femininity on the other, it is very difficult to resist this temptation. I wish to point out that exactly the same difficulty exists with regard to my two new terms. It would be so easy and so tempting to say that philobatism, aggressiveness, activity, and masculinity are closely related, in the same way as are apparently ocnophilia, masochism, passivity, and femininity. If one does not probe very far, many superficial arguments and observations can be adduced to support these two statements. In my opinion they will prove as correct—or as false—as the two three-cornered equations quoted at the beginning of this paragraph.

[1] S. Freud, 'Instincts and Their Vicissitudes' (1915), *Collected Papers*, Vol. IV.

V

LOVE AND HATE

THE words ocnophil and philobat were deliberately chosen so that each should contain the root 'phil', which means love. By this I wanted to call attention to the fact that to my mind the two states are not opposites, although at first glance they appear to be so. It would be easy to be misled by the fact that the ocnophil needs his objects and the philobat avoids them, or that the philobat loves his friendly expanses and the ocnophil abhors them, and to infer that either of these two sentiments is the negative of the other. A similar mistake was made in the beginnings of our theory of the instincts, when we assumed, for example, that sadism and masochism were true opposites. In order to avoid a repetition of this mistake, I must emphasise that ocnophilia and philobatism are not opposites; they are two different attitudes, possibly developing or, so to speak, branching off from the same stem.

Especially must I warn against considering one type as mainly loving and the other as mainly hating. This would be a gross mistake, as both types are loving and hating at the same time. What we must examine is what kind of love and what kind of hatred we encounter in each of the two types.

For instance the ocnophil, especially in moments of danger, has to have an object to cling to. It is true that the physical proximity, especially being in touch with the object, allays his fear, but does it necessarily follow from this that he loves the object? Quite often we find that the opposite is the case; for instance, that the ocnophil despises himself for his weakness, displaces this, and hates his object for his own dependence on it. This hatred may be so strong in some cases that after his fear has been allayed, in order to regain his self-respect, the ocnophil must abandon the object irrespective of the pain caused thereby to the object or to himself.

Similarly it would be easy to say that the philobat mistrusts and hates objects, as they represent unpredictable hazards for him. This, however, is only part of the truth, as for instance all the objects constituting his 'equipment', his 'gear', are dear and precious to him, and so are usually also the people who supply them. We have already discussed the unconscious meaning of these 'ocnophilic objects' as symbolic representations of the loving mother on the one hand and of the potent phallus on the other, both of them evoking highly positive emotions in the philobat. I have also mentioned the one attractive woman on the ground, helping and admiring the acrobat high in the air, and receiving him back with delight on his return. The same pattern was represented by the lady who gave a token to the knight-errant and waited patiently and lovingly for his return, a pattern still realised today both in poetry and in real life. But the beautiful, admiring, and patient lady of the safety zone is only one facet of a highly ambivalent situation. The other facet is the powerful attraction, both physical and psychological, of the safety zone—usually the earth—an attraction to which one must not abandon oneself, as the penalty is real mortal danger. (This is an eternal theme in folklore, literature, art—and acrobatics, just like its counterpart, the unconditionally loved ocnophilic object, dropping at a whim the credulous lover.)

Thus, both the ocnophil's and the philobat's relationship to his objects is ambivalent, loving and hating, trusting and mistrusting at the same time. Of course this could have been predicted, as both the ocnophil and the philobat, at any rate in the forms we have been able to study, are adults. The more we study adults, the more we recognise that being adult is tantamount to having ambivalent feelings. Moreover, as far as we can penetrate into childhood with our verbal analytical means, we always find ambivalence. This, too, was to be expected. Words are precipitates of experienced relationships to objects which made claims on us, which did not understand our needs unless we *told* them, 'in so many words', what our needs were. The great question is whether there is a pre-ambivalent phase at all. What we can confidently say is that if there is one, it must be definitely pre-verbal.

This question can be answered, as far as I can see, only by extrapolation; that is to say, by inference from data observed in adults and older children, to possible—or very probable—processes in pre-verbal infancy. This is, of course, a risky procedure, and before embarking upon it in Part II it is most advisable to make our starting platform as safe as possible. So before we leave the world of adults I propose to examine in the next chapter the ways and methods adopted by the ocnophil and by the philobat to justify their picture of the world.

VI

REALITY TESTING

IT is obvious that neither the philobat nor the ocnophil is fully justified in his picture of the world. They both rely on faults and omissions in their testing of reality. If it were not so, we should all enjoy—or abhor—in the same way the same pleasures and the same thrills.

We must now turn to the question of what enables one to maintain, against the testimony of one's experience, that there are people who hold the exactly opposite view—that, for instance, roundabouts are either highly enjoyable or, on the contrary, horrid. The answer is that to a certain extent everyone mixes up external reality with his own internal world; that is to say, we all take our reactions and attitudes at any one time as proper and trustworthy indicators of what actually is happening in the external world. It would be easy to call this mixing up of external and internal realities a survival from the narcissistic period which tries to form the world in its own image. Although to some extent this is true, our problem remains unanswered; we have still to find out how this faulty reality testing is possible and why it persists in an adult.

Here I wish to refer to my paper 'Contributions to Reality Testing',[1] in which I proposed to consider reality testing as occurring in steps. The first step is to decide whether a particular sensation is *coming from within or without*. The second step is to infer from the sensations what it is that causes them; this step may be called the *object formation*. Very closely connected with it is the third step—to find the significance of the sensation. The problem to be solved is: What does it

[1] *British Journal of Medical Psychology*, 1942, **19**, 201. (Reprinted in my *Problems of Human Pleasure and Behaviour*. London: Hogarth Press, 1957.)

mean to me that I perceive it? This step could be called the *interpretation* or *finding of the meaning*. The fourth step is then *to find the appropriate reaction* to the sensation perceived. It is important to bear in mind that steps 1 to 3 are almost independent of reality, as they cannot be checked by direct experience. This fact explains the parallel existence of different, even contradictory, religious, political, and even scientific opinions.

Of course, both the philobat and the ocnophil perform steps 1 and 2—deciding whether the sensations are coming from within or without and forming an object—in the same way. They have no difference of opinion on the fact that, for instance, roundabouts definitely are objects belonging to the external world. Where they differ is in the third step—the finding of the meaning, the interpretation, of their sensations. It is impossible to use any logical argument against their particular way of performing this third step of reality testing. The ocnophil's sensations are convincing, he really feels afraid or miserable whenever he is on a roundabout, so his inference is quite correct, roundabouts *are* horrid. But in the same way no logical argument can do anything about the philobat's inference from his own sensations, roundabouts *are* enjoyable and thrilling.

Moreover, for either of them there is very little possibility of any real change. Their experiences in this field are absolutely convincing, and if they repeat the experiences, they inevitably come to the same result, namely that roundabouts are horrid for the ocnophil and enjoyable and thrilling for the philobat. Of course, this is a typical case of mixing up the internal and the external worlds. The external world is exactly the same for both philobat and ocnophil. It is only their internal worlds that are different, and only if we succeed in changing them will the roundabouts and all the other thrills change from horrid to enjoyable, or the other way round. What the mechanisms and dynamics of such a change are will be discussed in my next book: *The Three Areas of the*

Mind. Here, however, I wish to emphasise that common everyday experience is unavailing; something different is needed for this change.

A further important point is that the psycho-analytic study of reality testing has been confined to a limited field, viz. that of practically unemotional perceptions and sensations. Yet we know that there is a further, equally important field in which reality testing of a kind has a paramount function—that is, the field of emotions, affects, and sentiments.

In the first approach one may be tempted to say that all feelings and emotions are real and therefore there is no need to test their reality. Some complication arises, however, when one takes into account that at times we pretend to feel in some way different from the way we actually feel. This pretence is often the result of conscious decision, but by no means always so. As everyone who has conducted analyses knows, people are often completely unaware that their honestly professed feelings and emotions are mainly pretences. In order to keep these potential pretences in check we must continually test the reality, not only of our sensations and perceptions but also of our emotions and feelings. This aspect might be called testing their sincerity or honesty. There are several complications facing us, however. It may now be taken as an established fact that the human mind consists of parts in very involved relation to one another. Some of the parts have already been studied, and even named; accordingly we speak of the superego, ego, and id; but also of internal objects, character, self; or again, using the oldest psycho-analytical terminology, of the conscious, preconscious, and unconscious, and so on. The interrelation of all these parts is anything but clear, but it is certain that a feeling, affect, or emotion may be sincere as far as one part is concerned, and a complete pretence for another. Here our theory has a good deal of leeway to make up.

There is yet another aspect of reality testing of emotions, and although the previous aspect has some bearing on our problem it is this latter that is of sterling importance for it. The question to be decided is whether or not our feelings, affects, and emotions are justified by external events and are appropriate reactions to them. Obviously our actions will be fundamentally influenced by the result of this kind of testing. I have already mentioned this problem in my paper on reality testing quoted above, as the fourth step. As far as I know, there is hardly any literature on this topic, but perhaps it may be hoped that a study of the philobatic and the ocnophilic pictures of the world may contribute something to its elucidation.

After this excursion into the uncharted lands of our theory, let us now return to the study of the faults in the reality testing of philobats and ocnophils. For the philobat reality testing is bi-phasic. In the 'home'—i.e. the zone of security—hardly any testing of any importance is needed, except perhaps for testing the sources for the acquisition of the 'right kind' of reliable equipment and gear. The philobat's attention may be turned inside, as instanced by so many morose, solitary, or brooding sailors and aircrews in port. Another type, equally frequent, is the over-elated one, always on the chase for easy pleasures. We may call this latter type either manic, over-compensating the underlying depression, or may suspect a forceful attempt to extend the rule of his philobatic world into the zone of security.

In the other phase—i.e. while enjoying thrills in the 'friendly expanses'—the testing of external reality must be most exacting. Often it is literally true that one false move may mean mortal danger; hence all the attention must be turned outside. Anxiety is aroused by the hazards represented by external objects and allayed by the achievement of overcoming them. There is very little relationship to these hazardous objects, certainly no concern about them, and consequently hardly any depression. In fact, a number of depressive people emerge from their black mood while in the mountains, or flying, racing, competing, on an expedition, etc. Possibly there is yet another factor that may contribute to their emergence from depression: in their 'friendly expanses' the philobats' cathexes are turned outward, away from their internal world which, thus, is—at any rate temporarily—out of any danger of being harmed or damaged.

The philobat viewed from this angle minimises the real dangers, even denies their existence. He seems to say, 'Leave it to me; I can deal with it'. In fact, his confidence is never fully justified. The real situation is well illustrated by a story. A man, doubtless an ocnophil, timidly inquires from the conductor before entering a cable cabin whether the cable is safe enough and what will happen if it breaks. The conductor tries to reassure him that there is a reserve cable, and that if that breaks there is even a second reserve. But the man goes on pestering, 'What if that too should break?' The answer is, 'Then you can go to hell'. A bystander, obviously a philobat, cannot refrain from remarking, 'I suggest you go to hell as soon as the first reserve cable breaks'. In fact, the anxious inquiry of the ocnophil is fully justified, and perhaps the philobat is a fool to accept unnecessary risks in his search for thrills. What justifies his confidence in himself, in his 'equipment', and in his friendly expanses? A confidence which may be expressed in phrases like: 'Things will turn out all right'; 'My return is safe'; etc.

We shall return to this question later after we have discussed the flaws in the ocnophil's reality testing. For him the spaces between objects are horrid and frightening, but the objects themselves are safe and protective. In a way this would seem to be sensible, but is it really so? Are all objects really always safe? Will the drowning man be saved by clutching at a straw? Obviously not; his salvation if in water will more likely depend on his ability to swim and to find a way out of the danger zone. What justifies the ocnophil's confidence in his objects? Or, to put the same question differently, what is the mechanism that enables him to believe that objects are safer than empty spaces?

Moreover, apart from the philobat's blind confidence in his ability to cope with hazards and in his safe homecoming, and the ocnophil's that objects are kind, safe, and protective, there is a further flaw in their attitudes towards the world. However long the philobat's sojourn in the friendly expanses, it is a transitory state; it *must* begin and end with objects however loath he may be to recognise and admit it. The approach to the home—airport, harbour, foot of a mountain, etc.—may be dangerous and may call for the utmost skill, but the home itself is protective and friendly and, above all, absolutely necessary. It is only in exceptional cases that philobats can sustain themselves by their own efforts in their exposed, thrilling zones; moreover, they almost always need the assistance of those unremembered or forgotten, but reliable, helpers who will be discussed in Chapter XIII.[1] And lastly, as we have seen, even in highly philobatic situations there is practically always some object, usually carried in the hand. Although this ocnophilic object is carefully disguised as 'equipment' or 'gear', it is easily recognisable as a symbolic representation of the safe home, the mother, on the one hand, and of the powerful phallus on the other.

I have mentioned on several occasions that the approach to the safe objects is often hazardous. I think that apart from its actual reality this danger has a powerful psychological determinant as well. This source of danger is the undeniable attraction of the objects, an attraction which the philobat usually minimises, ridicules, or denies. This denial is facilitated by a common displacement which enables him to say that the danger is in the object itself and not in the attraction

[1] The submarine service depends on volunteers, i.e. on philobats. They are the heroes. The unmentioned and often unremembered helpers live in the depot ship, called 'Mummy' all over the world. Jules Verne's hero, Captain Nemo, a real philobat with practically no objects, called his ship *Nautilus*. This was the name of the very first submarine ever built, and has been recently given to the first atomic submarine which, once equipped, does not need any helpful objects at all, and can cruise submerged practically indefinitely, limited only by the psychological endurance of her crew.

that it exerts on him. One very annoying form of this attraction engineers that mudguards—for some ununderstandable reason—get scratched and dented, and it is fair to say that garage doors, the entrance to the safe home, are perhaps the most dangerous, most attractive objects. There are also innumerable stories about the budding skier being irresistibly attracted by the one tree or bush standing forlorn in the middle of a vast field. In the same way, only in a much more tragic form, the pilot's most exacting task is taking off and landing his plane. It is a great day when a driver discovers that instead of anxiously watching the obstacles—i.e. objects —he can confidently head for the safe spaces between them.

Mutatis mutandis, something similar is true of the ocnophil. For him leaving the physical contact with his object is frightening, painful, almost unbearable. When playing football he keeps the ball too long; when driving he must hug the kerb or stick faithfully behind a slow-moving lorry; when ski-ing he dare not lean forward enough; when jumping he seems to stick to the ground, etc.; and it is well to remember that hesitating too long before crossing the road is almost as dangerous as rushing across.

Furthermore, the ocnophil is just as insincere to himself as the philobat. In the latter we found that behind the flaunting of his independence there exists, though carefully hidden, a real need for safe objects. Here we have the ocnophil finding security in physical proximity to his objects, but, we must ask, why does he cling to them so desperately? His desperate clinging is a reaction to a real or imaginary threat that somehow he may lose them. Either some brutal force may tear him away or, still more frightening, his object may become indifferent and carelessly, even maliciously, drop him. Like the philobat, the ocnophil too minimises or even denies the danger, and his denial is likewise facilitated by a common displacement which enables him to say that the danger is *not* in the object but outside it, and can be warded off if he can remain in touch with his object by clinging to it tightly.

THRILLS

We have met two problems. We found, on the one hand, that the philobat's confidence in his ability to cope with external dangers, in the friendliness of the expanses and in his safe homecoming, was exaggerated and somewhat unrealistic, and in the same way the ocnophil's belief that his objects were safe, powerful, and kind, was equally out of the true. We asked in the first paragraphs of this chapter what the mechanisms are enabling them to stick to their convictions in spite of the ubiquitous testimony of their experience, that other people have the extreme opposite view and events do not justify either of them. The search for the answers to these questions has led us to the assumption of a more primitive picture of the world which must be chronologically earlier than either the ocnophilic or the philobatic worlds. With this, however, we must leave the common conventional world of adults and enter the primitive world of early infancy and of regression.

PART II

Regressions

VII

OBJECT AND SUBJECT

OBJECT, and for that matter subject too, are not quite exact and rather aggressive renderings of much gentler, unaggressive Greek words. The Greek originals were created by the philosopher-grammarians of the Stoic school and, it should be added, rather late in the day. Almost all the classical Greek literature as we know it was already extant. The Homeric epics, the tragedies of Sophocles, Euripides, and Aeschylus, the comedies of Aristophanes, the histories of Thucydides and Xenophon, all the beautiful poetry of Pindar, Sappho, Anacreon, etc., even the dialogues of Plato, had long been written when Aristotle, and after him the Stoa, started to tidy up our ways of thinking and speaking about things and events. For them the main thing in any statement about an act or a state was the verb. The thing or person about which the statement was made was called τὸ ὑποκείμενον, which literally means 'that which lies under'. The Latin translation substituted 'being thrown' instead of 'lying', and created 'subject', literally meaning 'that which is thrown under' (an action or a statement). The other person or thing to which the action or statement extends was called τὸ ἀντικείμενον or τὸ προκείμενον, meaning literally 'that which lies against or athwart'. This was translated into Latin as 'object', in the same aggressive way, meaning, 'that which is thrown at or athwart' (an action or a statement).

All the European languages have simply borrowed the Latin terms, thus escaping the necessity of creating their own. The only exception I know of is Hungarian, which calls the object *tárgy*, which originally meant 'target', and it is possible that the two words have the same root. Moreover, both object and subject have further aggressive connota-

59

tions. According to the *Concise Oxford Dictionary*, 'to object' means 'to adduce as objection; state as damaging fact to or against a person, etc.; state objection; feel or express disapproval; have objection or dislike to, etc.'. 'To subject' means 'subdue, expose, treat'. 'Subject' as an adjective means 'under government, not independent, owing obedience, in subjection, liable or exposed to, etc.'.

Thus, 'object' seems to have two interrelated meanings. On the one hand, it denotes the target, determining by its attraction the direction of the action described by the verb of the sentence. It was this meaning which prompted Freud to choose this word to describe an important aspect of the instincts. In his *Three Essays on Sexuality*,[1] he tried to tidy up the field of the sexual instincts, using three criteria for classifying them. These are the aim, the object, and the source of an instinct. The source is the part of the body in which the instinctual urge is felt to originate; the aim is the act towards which the instinct tends; and lastly, the object is that part of the external world, usually a person, or of one's own body, from which the sexual attraction proceeds.

The other meaning of 'object' seems to be obstacle in the way of the action, in fact a resistant obstacle that has to be negotiated. If I remember rightly, A. McLeod in an unpublished paper entitled 'Embryology and Early Object Relations'[2] called our attention to the idea that perhaps our very first perceptions about objects may be those of resistance, i.e. something firm against which we may pitch our strength, either successfully or unsuccessfully. This conception is certainly in harmony with the cluster of associations surrounding the word 'object'.

According to this second, primitive, idea which, however, is still rampant even in our adult thinking and feeling, objects are something firm, sharply contoured, and resistant. In my paper on 'The Dissolution of Object Representation in

[1] (Standard ed., Vol. VII.) London: Hogarth Press, 1955.
[2] Read to the British Psycho-Analytical Society, January 17th, 1951.

Modern Art',[1] I discussed the fate of this idea in artistic creation. We may assume that an eternal ambition of art is to represent nature or life (which are meant to include the inner world of the artist) as faithfully and sincerely as possible. For quite a time nature—or life—was conceived as a collection or conglomeration of solid, separate, clearly defined and sharply contoured entities called objects. Science followed suit, and for some time conceived both the physical and the chemical worlds as consisting of firm, sharply contoured objects, the mechanical points, and the molecules or atoms. It is easy to show that this picture of the world is based partly on a psychological process—projection. We conceive the objects, the ultimate constituents of the world, as we wish to see ourselves, or perhaps even as we really see ourselves—firm, unchangeable, indestructible, in fact eternal. Since on this occasion we are concerned only with the primitive conceptions of subject and object, I will not follow up the various changes that object representation has had to undergo in recent centuries, either in science, in literature, or in art. To sum up, the meaning of 'object' as a resistant obstacle seems to be more primitive than that as an objective.

Liquids are not really objects and gases certainly are not. It was a later, more sophisticated way of thinking that was able to integrate these two states of matter with the solids in the general conception of objects. When attempting to include solids, liquids, and gases together, science and philosophy developed other words, such as substrate, substance, and matter. The first two are Latin, non-aggressive, variants of the already quoted Greek original τὸ ὑποκείμενον. Substrate is a comparative new-comer to the English language, and means literally 'that which is spread under'; substance, which is well established, means literally 'that which stands or is under'. They both mean roughly[2] the essential nature

---

[1] *Journal of Æsthetics and Art Criticism* (U.S.A.), **10**, No. 4, 1952. Reprinted in *Problems of Human Pleasure and Behaviour* (*op. cit.*).

[2] With due apology to philosophical exactitude.

underlying the accidental phenomena; or that which is regarded as supporting the attributes and accidents, that which receives modifications but is not itself a mode, that in which accidents or attributes inhere. And lastly, 'matter' derives from a common Indo-Germanic root denoting mother.

So far so good, but here we encounter our first problem. Parts of the external world which are felt to be firm, resistant, and sharply contoured are called by a special, somewhat aggressive, name—'object', which suggests both resistance against our wishes and aim or target for our strivings. Other parts of the same world, which are not solid, do not resist much, and have no real contours, are called by non-aggressive names, such as substance, substrate, both showing similarity to 'subject' denoting ourselves. A third, very generally used, word—matter—describing these not so sharply contoured, less resistant parts of the world, derives from a root denoting mother. The inescapable inference is that at one time there must have been a harmonious mix-up in our minds between ourselves and the world around us, and that our 'mother' was involved in it. Though this mix-up strikes us as childish and primitive, we must admit that it preceded our 'modern', 'adult', or 'scientific' picture of the world which, so to speak, grew out of it, and undeniably some of its primitive features were carried over into its later form.

Before discussing what psycho-analysis can contribute to the understanding of this development, I wish to mention that the physiological psychology of the senses is in full agreement with the idea of the secondary nature of objects. I think it is generally agreed that, ontogenetically, sharply contoured objects emerge only gradually out of a matrix—another suspiciously primitive word deriving from 'mother'. The two most important senses that provide the perceptions which form the basis for the discovery of 'objects' are sight and touch. Both of them are undeveloped in the first post-natal months, as they need a considerable degree of muscular co-ordination to work properly; as is well known, binocular vision does not exist in the first weeks of life. Moreover, both sight and touch, together with hearing, are projective senses; they feel, place, or construct the object outside the body, either at a distance (sight and hearing) or at its surface (touch).

The situation is utterly different with the two lower senses, which are well, perhaps even fully, operative at birth. In their function there is hardly any projection; we feel smell and taste inside our body—*in* our mouth or *in* our nose; moreover, the sensations themselves, more often than not, have nothing to do with objects, only with substances. Here we get some idea how and why the mix-up between ourselves and the world around us has come about. Looking at it as an external detached observer, we recognise that it is based on an interaction between the individual and the external world; one may say that the world has intruded or penetrated into the individual's mouth or nose, and equally correctly that the individual has taken in parts of the external world— penetrated into it.

The same kind of mix-up occurs with the sense of temperature, though to a lesser degree. In fact, it forms a transition between the lower and the higher senses, i.e. those based on mix-up and those using projection. Cold and warmth are felt partly as coming from outside, partly as a state of our own body or even of ourselves: *we* feel warm or *it* is warm. Concurrently any object, if it is recognisable at all on the basis of temperature sensations alone, is felt or construed only in a hazy and vague way.

This mixing-up of the external and the internal worlds is well known in psycho-analysis, and has been studied from various angles for various purposes, though a systematic study of this topic has not yet been undertaken. First there exist a number of clinical phenomena in which the boundary between the two worlds becomes blurred or even disappears; these are: illusion and hallucination, confusion, fugues, depersonalisation, not forgetting the toxic states caused by drugs. Then there are the two important dynamic processes: projection and introjection; roughly speaking, we tend to behave as if everything good were in us—introjection—and everything painful or objectionable in the external world— projection. Though checked to a large extent by the function of reality testing, these tendencies remain active as long as we live; true, they soon become complicated by secondary processes, and the ultimate picture is anything but simple and transparent. Although these processes are most important for our topic, as well as for psycho-analytic technique, I wish to confine myself to another field—the emergence of objects and its effect on the mind.

This proposition may sound somewhat fantastic. After all, the people we analyse—no matter whether patients or candidates who are training for psycho-analysis, adults or children —are all well beyond the time when objects were being discovered. This is true, but during psycho-analytic treatment a curious process takes place, called regression. What emerges from the study of regression in the psycho-analytic situation is that all of us have a fantasy of a primal harmony which by right ought to be our due and which was destroyed either through our own fault, through the machinations of others, or by our cruel fate. It is impossible to get an accurate description of this state apart from that in it all of our wishes will be automatically satisfied; in fact, we shall feel no want. (The verbs of this sentence are in the future tense; equally correctly they could be in the past or present tense, or in all three tenses at the same time—a good illustration of the impossibility of obtaining an accurate description.) This harmony is the theme of a number of religious beliefs and fairy tales, and appears to be the ultimate goal of all human striving. This striving for a complete harmony between the subject and his environment may be approximated (a) in our sexual life, in particular in its most intense phase— during orgasm, and (b) in all forms of ecstasy. Perhaps the most important quality of all these states—fairy tales, ecstasies, sexual orgasm—is an almost complete identity between the individual and his environment, i.e. between the microcosmos and the macrocosmos.

The fact that it is impossible to get a proper description of these states points to the possibility that they belong to a period in which words did not yet exist. In psycho-analysis three theories have been developed to explain these states; in some way they contradict, in another they complement one another. These three theories are: (1) *primary narcissism*, according to which all emotional interest was centred originally on oneself, and only later experiences forced or enticed the individual to detach some of his love from himself and turn it towards part of his environment. (2) The theory of *absolute omnipotence* is thought to be a kind of second stage to primary narcissism. According to this the infant, provided he is nursed fairly efficiently, lives in an hallucination that as soon as he experiences a need or a wish it will be immediately satisfied because his wishes, or he himself, are omnipotent. (3) The third theory is that of *primary object-relationship or primary love*, which maintains that a healthy child and a healthy mother are so well adapted to each other that the same action inevitably brings gratification to both. Good examples are sucking—feeding, cuddling—being cuddled, and so on. Thus for some time a healthy infant feels that there is no difference of interest—in fact not much difference of any kind—between himself and his environment, that is he and his environment are mixed up.

According to the theory of primary narcissism, in the first phases of life there is no experience of an external world, only of the self. The theory of primary omnipotence allows a hazy notion of something beyond the self, but there is no idea of harmony between the beyond and the self, only of automatic, instantaneous satisfaction. The theory of primary love presupposes the experiencing of an external world, but it assumes that there exists a harmony between the individual and his world; that is, there is not—and cannot be—any clash of interest between the two. Obviously this state is nearest to the mix-ups that we discussed earlier in this section. A good example in adult life of this primary state is our relationship to the air surrounding us. We use it for our own ends, inhale and exhale it, take parts out of it that we need and put other parts into it that we want to get rid of, without paying the least attention or consideration to it, without even noticing its existence. In fact, it would be a somewhat comical question to inquire whether the air likes or does not like our use of it. It must be there because we simply cannot live without it.

By the way, the air is not an object but a substance. Further, it must be pointed out that there is no need to define exact boundaries at which the external air stops and we ourselves start. In fact, it would be a kind of hairsplitting to do so, as it would amount only to a play with words to ask, for instance, whether the air contained in our lungs is part of ourselves or part of the external world. Obviously it is both, it is a mix-up. Almost the same is true, by the way, of the contents of our bowels. In some way they are our 'inside' in the strictest sense of the word; in another way they belong to the external world though undeniably they are inside us.

May I add that this neither-here-nor-there psychological state is reciprocated by the embryology and histology of the same organs? Both the intestines and lungs are lined with a special kind of epithelium which is contiguous with the skin that covers our body; moreover, though it is morphologically different, embryologically it is a derivative of it. So here, too, we have a kind of mix-up between outside and inside; at any rate, the boundaries are so uncertain and vague that it is hardly possible to say where inside ends and outside begins. This could be continued by quoting further instances of the uncertain morphological or physiological boundaries in our body.

Through our clinical experiences we have arrived at a

primitive picture of the world in which (*a*) there is complete harmony between individual and environment; (*b*) the individual does not care and is not in a position to say where he ceases and the external world begins; and (*c*) neither can an external observer define exact boundaries. At this stage of development there are as yet no objects, although there is already an individual, who is surrounded, almost floats, in substances without exact boundaries; the substances and the individual mutually penetrate each other; that is, they live in a harmonious mix-up.

Apart from love and mystical ecstatic experience, it is only in poetry, in fiction, and in art that an individual and an important part of his environment—i.e. things external to him—may become one and the same thing. The English language has an admirable expression for this exceptional coincidence; it speaks of the 'subject-matter' of a poetic or artistic creation. This would seem to be an impossible contradiction; the subject cannot be a matter, and matter cannot be subjective. Still it beautifully describes the something, which is both inside and outside the confines of an individual, which is both himself and part of his 'friendly expanses' and out of which something might be created—in fact a mix-up.

In psycho-analytic theory we are wont to classify mother's milk among the earliest objects, but it is arguable whether milk, a liquid, is ever considered to be an object by an unprejudiced, common-sense man. One cannot reject out of hand the suspicion that the idea of milk as an object emerged in the minds of sophisticated analysts and not necessarily in the minds of infants. If I am right, milk would be another instance of the friendly expanse with no objects in it, a matter, a substance. If we accept this, then the widespread inexplicable fads in many people about the skin in milk might be understood. The skin is a hazardous object appearing in the 'substance' milk, painfully disturbing the primitive harmony.

The discovery that firm and separate independent objects

exist destroys this world. From then on, in addition to substances, the existence of objects with their resistant, aggressive, and ambivalent qualities must be accepted. Despite many gradations and shades, there are apparently two basic ways in which people respond to this traumatic discovery. One is to create an ocnophilic world based on the phantasy that firm objects are reliable and kind, that they will always be there when one needs them, and that they will never mind and never resist being used for support. The other is to create the philobatic world which goes back to life prior to the experience that objects emerge and destroy the harmony of the limitless contourless expanses. Objects are felt as dangerous and unpredictable hazards, or as equipment to be picked up or dispensed with. This world is coloured by an unjustified optimism—originating in the earlier world of primary love—that enables the philobat to believe that his skills and his equipment will be sufficient to cope with the elements—the substances—as long as he can avoid hazardous objects.

This train of thought could explain why an ambivalent name was given to objects. They are, in fact, 'objectionable' for the philobat and 'objectives' for the ocnophil. It also explains the fact that languages need two kinds of words for describing the external world, one class of them more distant from the term used to denote ourselves, the subject, and another closely related to it, including one derived from 'mother'. Whereas the first class of words is reserved to describe firm, resistant, and sharply contoured parts of the external world with which no mix-up is possible, the latter class is reserved for the limitless substances and the friendly expanses.

The history of the concepts of the physical world around us gives us a very interesting and highly instructive parallel to the antithesis between the philobatic and ocnophilic worlds. The controversial ideas about the world can be classified in two patterns. One is the atomic conception, according to which everything consists of small, firm, and resistant little objects, moving at high speed and knocking against one another constantly—a theory starting with Demokritos and reaching its culmination perhaps in the classical kinetic theory of gases and the Rutherford-Bohr model of the atom. The other idea is that of an all-embracing continuum, also originating with the early Greek philosophers, and culminating in the perhaps defunct theory of the all-pervading ether, and the modern theory of the electron which is so diffuse that at any one time it may be at any one point of its shell. The parallel is still more exact, as according to the theory of ether the atoms were considered as discontinuities in the continuous ether, as, so to speak, holes or whirls in it—clearly a philobatic conception.

VIII

FLYING DREAMS AND
THE DREAM SCREEN

I WISH to emphasise that—with the exception of the theoretical discussion in the previous chapter—up to this point only experiences with grown-ups have been used. Conversely this means that all the observations on which my arguments have been based belong to the verbal period, and thus can be easily verified or refuted by analytic practice. It is only at this point that I have to go farther, and use my findings to infer from them what might happen in pre-verbal periods— that is, in early childhood and in deeply regressed states.

This is a more uncertain, more controversial, field, as we all know. The cause of this uncertainty is the dependence of the subject, baby or patient, on his environment—that is, on the observer. In both situations—earliest childhood, highly regressed patient—the dependence on the environment is an essential factor, and if we were to try to avoid or overcome it we should destroy exactly what we set out to observe. Conversely it means that a highly important constituent of what we observe is our own contribution. Moreover, the younger the baby, the more regressed the patient, the more important we are for him, and the greater will be the influence of our emotional participation, and of our theoretical expectations, on what will happen in these highly dependent states. An awkward enough situation, which is made still more awkward by the fact that the most important part of our contribution inevitably comes from our own unconscious. Being scientifically detached or consciously controlled may thwart, by the lack of emotional spontaneity, the development of the very thing we want to observe; on the other hand, being led by our unconscious expectations and not keeping an eye on our repressed instinctual urges, which might easily get stirred up by someone so completely dependent on us, we may be induced to find confirmations by creating them ourselves.

In addition, the young baby and the regressed patient live in a pre-verbal state, and thus we, who set out to be emotionally uninvolved scientific observers, become not only participants and partners but also interpreter-informants, and finally translators. This, too, is an unavoidable complication, as pre-verbal experiences constitute the main interests of these situations. It is we who have to put into adult, scientifically correct, words emotional expressions which have not yet settled down to a conventional vocabulary or an easily recognisable grammar. By vocabulary I mean the set of technical terms familiar to the observer, and by grammar the mental mechanisms which, according to his theory, regulate and explain these primitive processes. Obviously very few technical terms or theoretical explanations will be used in the nursery or in the analyst's consulting-room, perhaps even none at all; still, every utterance, communication, sign of understanding, or of lack of understanding on the observer's part will be influenced by this kind of vocabulary and grammar—just as much as our speech and thinking is determined by our mother tongue.

Inevitably both the vocabulary and the grammar used to describe the experiences in these states will be our own. Anyone who has tried to express in one adult language ideas conceived in another knows how much gets lost from, and how much has to be added to, the original in order to make it understandable in its second garb. The more emotionally charged the communication the more difficult the translation becomes, as is convincingly demonstrated by the well-nigh impossibility of translating true lyric poetry. Now experiences in pre-verbal states, either infantile or regressed, are of necessity highly emotionally charged and—to make things still more difficult—have as yet not even been expressed in any adult language.

And lastly, in addition to our being participating partners, interpreter-informers, and translators, we end up by becoming with equal inevitability educators and teachers as well. Both the baby and the regressed patient in the end have no choice but to learn to speak the language—i.e. vocabulary and grammar—of the adult on whom they are dependent, the baby for his life, the regressed patient for his restoration.

To show the difficulties facing a research worker studying the phenomena of these primitive states how much his own personality will influence the ways in which he describes his experiences, may I quote Freud and the history of the flying dreams. Freud is still unsurpassed as a source of information for personal involvement. After innumerable similar experiences, it is still profoundly moving to encounter again and again his apparently merciless scientific honesty and unlimited sincerity. From his descriptions we can clearly see what it was that he observed and what motives led him to describe it in that particular way.

As early as the first edition of his *The Interpretation of Dreams*, Freud mentioned that a number of people have dreams of flying through the air. Freud called these dreams *Flugträume*. This description is rather misleading, as in such dreams no effort at all is experienced, the locomotion happens with the greatest of ease, in a most pleasant form, and immediately if any wish for it is experienced. A better description would be 'floating dreams', as the experience of weight to be carried, to be moved, is completely or almost completely absent. Freud classed these dreams among the typical dreams which 'presumably arise from the same sources in every case' (p. 241).[1] This common source, according to Freud, is to be found in childhood games, 'involving movements which are extraordinarily attractive to children' (p. 393). In later editions, to this source were added the sensations of erection and memories of the primal scene (p. 272). Although it was

[1] This and the following quotations are from S. Freud, *The Interpretation of Dreams* (Standard ed., Vols. IV and V). London: Hogarth Press, 1953.

Freud who first pointed out that water in dreams symbolically represents birth and intra-uterine existence, he never—so far as I know—related the flying dreams and intra-uterine existence to each other.

Characteristically he recorded frankly that he personally had no experience of such dreams; a fact which now we might possibly bring into connection with his well-known slight anxiety neurosis, especially his *Reisefieber*. This lack of direct experience might contribute also to the explanation of the curious history of the passages describing these dreams in the subsequent editions of *The Interpretation of Dreams*. First they were printed in Chapter V, Section D; then, after some additions, transferred to Chapter VI, Section E; and lastly, since the 1930 edition, in *both* places, although in somewhat different forms. (See *op. cit.*, pp. xiii and 271, Editor's notes.)

A further important point is that although in 1930—for the last time—Freud revised the whole book and especially Chapters V and VI, he did not consider it necessary to mention the ideas published in Ferenczi's *Thalassa*[1] in 1924, which threw new light on the *Flugträume*, although on any other point of the book Freud conscientiously recorded every important new contribution made by analysts.

Perhaps we can obtain some enlightenment on why all this happened from Freud's personal attitude to the 'oceanic' feeling which he described in 1928. Relating it to a suggestion by Romain Rolland, Freud wrote: 'This consists of a peculiar feeling, which never leaves him [i.e. Romain Rolland] personally, which he finds shared by many others, and which he may suppose millions more also experience. It is a feeling which he would like to call a sensation of "eternity", a feeling as of something limitless, unbounded, something "oceanic". It is, he says, a purely subjective experience, not an article of belief' (p. 8).[2]

---

[1] *Psa. Quarterly*, New York, 1938. German original, 1924.

[2] This and the following quotations from S. Freud, *Civilisation and its Discontents*. London: Hogarth Press, 1930.

Freud adds that he cannot discover this oceanic feeling in himself, and then proceeds to describe it somewhat ironically in his own words: 'If I have understood my friend aright he means the same thing as that consolation offered by an original and somewhat unconventional writer to his hero, contemplating suicide: "Out of this world we cannot fall."[1] So it is a feeling of indissoluble connection, of belonging inseparably to the external world as a whole' (p. 9).

Freud proposes a theory to explain why this feeling may persist in many people throughout their lives. Although in normal adults the ego is felt as having clear boundaries both inwards and outwards, this is not quite true. Inwards the boundary towards the id is anything but clear, and there are many conditions both physiological and pathological in which the external boundary tends to become uncertain or even to disappear. (See Chapter VII.) Freud quotes, as a physiological example, the state of being in love, which at its height 'threatens to obliterate the boundaries between ego and object. Against all the evidence of his senses the man in love declares that he and his beloved are one, and is prepared to behave as if it were a fact' (pp. 10 and 11). He then concludes: 'Originally the ego includes everything, later it detaches from itself the external world. The ego-feeling we are aware of now is thus only a shrunken vestige of a far more extensive feeling—a feeling which embraced the universe and expressed an inseparable connection of the ego with the external world. If we may suppose that this primary ego-feeling has been preserved in the minds of many people—to a greater or lesser extent—it would co-exist like a sort of counterpart with the narrower and more sharply outlined ego-feeling of maturity, and the ideational content belonging to it would be precisely the notion of limitless extension and oneness with the universe—the same feeling as that described by my friend as "oceanic" ' (pp. 13 and 14). Freud

[1] Christian Grabbe, *Hannibal*: 'Ja, aus der Welt werden wir nicht fallen. Wir sind einmal darin.'

traces this feeling of oneness with the universe back to the baby at its mother's breast, but apparently considers it in an adult as an out-of-date remnant which should really be recognised as such and relegated from the present adult world to the memories of the infantile past. I think this demand is rather exacting. We get a hint of why Freud had to adopt such an exacting attitude towards this kind of experience when we follow his argument in the first chapter of *Civilisation and its Discontents*. At one point he derives the oceanic feeling from the situation of the baby in its mother's arms (p. 12), at another from the child's need for its father's protection (p. 21). It is not far-fetched to see in this vacillation the working of a strong ambivalence conflict which explains why the whole idea had to be minimised and pushed out of focus, and also why Freud was not able to settle the symbolism of the *Flugträume* in the various editions of his *Interpretation of Dreams*. Nowadays I think it will be accepted as self-evident that the flying dreams and the oceanic feeling are to be regarded as repetition either of the very early mother-child relationship or of the still earlier intra-uterine existence, during which we were really one with our universe and were really floating in the amniotic fluid with practically no weight to carry.

Of course I was very pleased to note that when discussing the flying dreams or the oceanic feeling Freud mentioned all the instances—except one—that build up my theory of primary love. These are: the baby in its mother's arms, being in love, floating, feeling of oneness with the universe. The one that he disregarded is clinical experiences with highly regressed patients, a topic he never liked much and to which we shall return presently. Before doing so I wish to round off the history of the floating dreams.

It was Ferenczi who made the next step in the interpretation of these dreams, in his *Thalassa*. He used the floating dreams, the well-known symbolism of water, the symbolical identity of baby and penis, and the feeling of oneness with one's environment, together as the starting-point of his phylo-genetic theory of coitus. If we accept all these suggestions, then the three states—the child safely held in its mother's arms, the intra-uterine, and the thalassal existence—are to be considered as symbolically identical; the friendly expanses of my theory are then but wish-fulfilling memories of these states; conversely, these states activate a strong attraction for regression and the ideational content of this tendency to regress is the concept of the friendly expanses, or—after repression and with a negative sign—that of the horrid empty spaces.

In support of the statement that the relation to concrete particular objects is secondary to an overriding, more primi-tive, relationship to the undifferentiated friendly expanses, in addition to those referred to in Chapter VII, further argu-ments can be brought also from physiological optics. When one shuts one's eyes one experiences something roughly hemi-spherical, surrounding one safely, the colour of which is grey if the intensity of light impinging on the eyelids is slight or pink if the intensity is considerable. This eye-grey or eye-pink, as it is called in physiological optics, is at a distance from us, but it is impossible to state with certainty whether it is outside or inside of us or, in fact, whether it is nearer or farther away than any given object. To my mind the eye-grey or eye-pink is a clear instance of the friendly expanses, their harmony as yet undisturbed by any object, or, in other words, although there are no objects in it, it is not a 'horrid empty space', it is friendly. Recently Bertram Lewin[1] published very interesting ideas on the dream screen which is doubtless a counterpart in the dreaming state of the eye-grey when awake. (It should be mentioned that, perhaps because the intensity of light striking the lids is minimal during sleep, most dreams are grey in grey; coloured dreams are excep-tional, the most frequent colour being red, corresponding to the eye-pink.) Biased by our prevailing theories, Lewin

[1] *Psychology of Elation*. London: Hogarth Press, 1951.

76

accepted one of its determinants as a complete explanation and identified the dream screen with the mother's breast. This explanation, although unassailable, is not the whole truth if seen from the point of view of the friendly expanses as advocated in this paper.

IX

THE CHRONOLOGY OF OCNOPHILIA AND PHILOBATISM

BEARING in mind the inevitable uncertainties inherent in any verbal description by an adult 'scientific' observer of these primitive pre-verbal states, in particular of earliest infancy, let us return to our main topic. What we have to discuss now are two interrelated questions. The one asks what the mechanisms are that enable the philobat and the ocnophil to distort their reality testing so as to be able to stick to their respective pictures of the world despite the everyday experience that the opposite type feels just the contrary; to some extent this was discussed in Chapter VI. The related question is, which of the two pictures of the world is chronologically the earlier, i.e. which developed out of which?

At first thought one would say that the ocnophilic world is the earlier of the two. We find that clinging to objects which may represent the mother is understandable, simple, and entails hardly any, or only very primitive, reality testing. Moreover, there is no need to rely on oneself, one accepts every not impossible object as representing the safe, good mother, and shies away from the horrid empty spaces where there is no good mother. The apparent primitiveness of this situation should not deter us from examining it in detail. Clinging presupposes the discovery, however dim, of objects which are firm and resistant. Very likely at first they are only parts which, however, must be preserved at all costs as they have a tendency to disappear, to abandon or drop one. Clinging is therefore both an expression of an anxiety and an attempt to prevent its outbreak. Thus the ocnophilic world appears to be another instance of the impotent omnipotence,[1]

[1] See 'Love and Hate' in *Primary Love and Psycho-Analytic Technique*.

a fantasy mobilised to save some scanty remnants of the earlier state of primary love. After the traumatic experience that objects, especially the good mother, might drop him, the clinging child accepts the fact that vitally important but inscrutable objects *do* exist outside him; but he pretends—in his impotent omnipotence—that they will never leave him if only he can attach himself inseparably to them. His reality testing does not compel him to acquire much personal skill apart from an efficient way of clinging and perhaps—although later in adult life this is hardly ever openly admitted—a costly method for being accepted by his objects as a kind of clinging parasite.

The apparently primitive situation of clinging is not so simple after all. There is still another complicating factor present. This is that by clinging one gets farther and farther away from the satisfaction of the original need, which was to be held safely. The profoundly tragic situation is that the more efficiently one clings, the less is one held by the object. (This ever-repeated experience during analytic treatment had a large share in building up our theories of ambivalence and frustration.) There are in the main two ways in which the ocnophil copes with this insoluble problem. Both of these use magical thinking. One method is for the ocnophil to project himself into the object and pretend that he himself is now as safely held as he can hold on to his object. This mechanism may explain a number of queer attitudes towards one's cherished possessions. The second and perhaps somewhat later method is for the ocnophil to introject his object, thus reassuring himself by this magical self-deception that now his object can never leave him, as it is inside him.

Both of these methods are, of course, mere magic acts which change only one's internal world but have no effect on external reality. In fact, the whole ocnophilic sphere is largely based on this kind of magical thinking which equips the objects with fantastic qualities, pretending that some objects are extremely good, benign, and helpful, and others, or even the same ones, are extremely bad, malicious, and hostile. Seen from this angle, ocnophilic thinking is primitive, certainly more primitive than the sentiments described by 'concern', 'regard', 'consideration', and especially by 'looking after' (see Chapter III). Perhaps this more primitive nature of the whole ocnophilic attitude is the reason why, so far as I know, no language has words to describe it.

In this ocnophilic world, as distinct from the world of concern, regard, etc., objects are only dimly perceived as real whole objects—i.e. as separate from me—because if they were separate they could drop or leave me, which in this state would be a truly major traumatic disaster. Perhaps the fact that we have no words to name these states is a kind of avoidance magic; what cannot be described by words cannot change, must remain the same for ever. This is the case with God's name in Hebrew, of which only the consonants and not the vowels are known.

In the same way as at first glance the ocnophilic attitude impressed us as very primitive, the philobatic attitude appears as highly developed. In a superficial way this impression is correct. The philobat has accepted reality, i.e. the separate existence of objects. Moreover, he is trying—to use two beautiful common English phrases—to see the world 'in its true perspective', 'in the correct proportions', all of which is much more than an ocnophil need do. And lastly, the philobat can feel 'concern' for objects that are at a distance from him, can occasionally even 'look after' them or is able to avoid them if he 'considers' them as hazards. Both these functions—concern for good, avoidance of hazardous objects —need *skill*.

I shall now try to describe what I mean by this skill, which signifies in the first instance the ability to deal with real external situations, i.e. a kind of adaptability to reality. Perhaps the first condition for acquiring this ability is an emotional acceptance of the depression caused by the realisation that objects are separate and independent from us. As we all know, magic is not reality; it is wish-fulfilment irrespective of reality. The change from fantasy and magic to testing the reality is the second step in adaptation to reality, some aspects of which I discussed in Chapter VI.

The third aspect of this adaptation is finding a roundabout way of gratifying the original need. Here various possibilities offer themselves. One is what I have described[1] as active love or conquering the object, i.e. changing it from an indifferent and unconcerned object into a co-operative partner. The various object-related instincts demand a varying degree of collaboration from the partner, e.g. oral and anal instincts demand less; genital instinct—especially in its most highly developed, most complicated form, in genital love— demands a collaboration from the object amounting to an almost complete identification with the subject; I differentiated this more developed form from the more primitive and less exacting oral identification, as genital identification.

Another form of these roundabout ways is conquering oneself. This leads to various narcissistic attitudes and auto-erotic gratifications. A third form is sublimation. This means the creation, in place of our faithless original objects, of new ones, or the acceptance as objects for our love and hate of things that have but little in common with our original ones. In some instances of sublimation the self is taken as object, as happens in dancing, acting, etc.

Apart from internal processes, all these activities or attitudes—active love, conquering oneself, sublimation—presuppose the acquisition of personal skills, which conversely means a high degree of reality testing and inevitably a continuous, searching self-criticism. In highly philobatic situations this never-relaxing self-criticism is literally vitally necessary, because the penalty for failure may be severe injury or even death. But even under less stringent conditions any 'false step' may have dire consequences.

This personal skill is the essence of philobatism: no philo-

[1] See 'Genital Love' in *Primary Love and Psycho-Analytic Technique*.

batism without skill. The ultimate aim of the philobat, however, is to master the task so completely and with such ease that the skill should no longer require any effort. I think, viewing the philobat's achievement from this angle, his is a case of the return of the repressed. After this consummate skill has been attained, reality may change into a kind of fairyland where things happen as desired, apparently demanding hardly any, or even no, effort from the philobat.

Some people will perhaps still remember the masterly Rastelli, who put up his little finger, and any ball thrown at him just stopped as a matter of course at the tip of his finger. It made no difference whether it was himself, his assistant, or someone from the stalls, or someone from the gallery who threw the ball; the ball stopped where Rastelli wanted it to, on the tip of his nose, on his shoulder, on his heel, in the middle of his back, or on the end of a stick which he held between his teeth. As seen on the stage, in the magic fairyland created by his exquisite skill, for Rastelli the balls were no longer separate entities; they flew where he wanted them to go and stopped where he wanted them to be.

What Rastelli achieved in an exquisite way in his world on the stage is achieved in a modest way by every philobat in his field. This kind of apparently effortless accomplishment which we admire in figure-skaters, in dancers, in actors, musicians, high-board divers, and so on, is also our own aim in our limited spheres of, say, driving a car, of ballroom dancing, or even merely of proper society manners.

To change the field, a similar fairyland of apparently effortless achievements may develop in a harmonious love relation based on far-reaching mutual genital identification as referred to above. The partners are there for each other when, where, and how they are wanted. The precondition of this high standard of achievement, both in physical reality and in love, is the acquisition of skill. The aim of this consummate skill is to re-create in reality something of the harmony that existed before the discovery of separate objects, the harmony of the friendly expanses holding and embracing one safely.

So far so good, but the philobat's behaviour in his 'friendly expanses' is highly suspect of being unjustifiably and primitively confident, in the same way as the ocnophil's behaviour was towards his objects. The philobat apparently firmly believes that his skill will be sufficient to cope with all hazards and dangers, and that everything will turn out all right in the end. It is up to him to conquer the world, but he is confident that his skill will be sufficient and that the world will not mind being conquered, will 'click in' with him.[1]

The philobatic world, therefore, is yet another example of not fully justified omnipotence, based again on regression.

---

[1] This kind of confidence is admirably described in a passage by Thomas Mann in the fourth volume of his *Joseph and His Brethren* ('Joseph the Provider'; London: Secker & Warburg, 1945). Once again Joseph had been too confident, forgot about the 'true perspective'; in fact, had blundered. His false step was followed inevitably by corresponding punishment: Potiphar cast him out and sent him to Zawi-Re as a convict slave for hard labour. Arriving he stood there waiting for the Commandant of the prison who was reading Potiphar's letter with the instructions. A grim situation, still Joseph was confident: 'His real confidence, however, was more of a generalization: it proceeded, as it is wont to do with children of the blessing, not from himself outwards but inwards upon himself and the happy mysteries of his own nature. Certainly he had got beyond the childish stage of blind confidence, where he had believed that everybody must love him more than they did themselves. What he continued to believe was that it was given him to constrain the world and the men in it to turn him their best and brightest side—and this we can see was confidence rather in himself than in the world. In any case the two, his ego and the world, in his view belonged together, they were in a way one, so that the world was not simply the world, by and in itself, but quite definitely his world and by virtue of the fact susceptible of being moulded into a good and friendly one. Circumstances were powerful; but what Joseph believed in was their plasticity; he felt sure of the preponderant influence of the individual destiny upon the general force of circumstances. When like Gilgamesh he called himself a glad-sorry man, it was in the sense that he knew the happy side of his nature was capable of much suffering, but on the other hand did not believe in suffering—bad and black enough it was that it had proved too dense for his own light, or the light of God in him, to penetrate. Such was the nature of Joseph's confidence.'

In this case, however, the regression seems to be going farther back than the discovery of the existence of separate, individual objects. By using extrapolation we may infer that this world is that of a structureless, primitive state, where there are as yet no, or only very few and unimportant, unpredictable objects, a world which consists only of kindly substances, constituting the friendly expanses, as described in Chapter III. This attitude is possibly the most primitive form of relation to the world, and may perhaps be represented, from the point of view of an outside observer, by the mother safely holding her baby, or—if we accept parallels from onto- and phylogenesis—as our ancestors in phylogenesis were safely held by the sea, or as we ourselves in our ontogenetic past were held by the amniotic fluid in our mother's womb. The philobat regresses in his fantasy to this conception of the world. He firmly believes that the friendly expanses will encompass him safely, just as he was held before the appearance of the untrustworthy and treacherous objects.

In order to be able to indulge in this fantasy, however, he must acquire a very high degree of personal skill, and must submit his performance to incessant, exacting reality testing, and to searching self-criticism. Perhaps the first such physical skill, and certainly the prototype for all the later ones, is the erect gait as distinct from crawling on all fours. It has in itself in rudimentary forms all the elements of the later thrills: letting go of the object, entering the spaces between objects, raising oneself away both from mother and from the safe earth, maintaining only precarious contact with the latter through the soles of one's feet, and above all developing a fine co-ordination for keeping equilibrium. As everyday experience shows, this is rather a difficult task for most children, and it is only after several months of experimenting and constant practice that they develop from crawling to waddling, from waddling to proper walking. It is easy to observe that in the first stages of learning to walk they throw themselves from object to object, cutting their sojourn in the unsafe empty spaces as short as possible; that is to say, behaving in a truly ocnophilic way. It is only when they have acquired some proficiency that they can enjoy the friendly expanses; i.e. can regress by progression.

The philobatic conception of the world is thus a queer mixture indeed. One component of this mixture is an exacting adaptation to external reality, requiring sustained effort, painstaking attention to details and, above all, searching self-criticism. The other component is self-abandonment to a somewhat unrealistic fantasy, presuming friendliness where in fact only indifference exists. The underlying fantasy probably is that the whole world, apart from the few accidental hazards, is a kind of loving mother holding her child safely in her arms or, phylogenetically, the structureless sea offering the same friendly environment in limitless expanses.

X

PROGRESSION FOR THE
SAKE OF REGRESSION

THIS mixture could be called regression by progression or progression for the sake of regression. In the case of the philobat the progression is the acquisition of the consummate skill necessary for dealing with reality. The aim of this progression, of the acquisition of the skill by unrelenting effort and self-criticism, is to enable one to regress to the state which may be described as in a way forgetting altogether about the world around onself; enjoying the harmony between oneself and one's environment. This state is obviously a denial of any separate existence. It may correctly be described—in a somewhat complicated way—as a simultaneous introjective identification with the partner and projective identification of the partner with oneself. But at the same time it is obviously also a regression to the state of primary love, to the undisturbed harmony, to the complete identity of subject and object, described in Chapter VII. Lastly, it is equally a progression to the acquisition of a skill in order to induce the object or even the whole actual world to accept the role of a co-operative partner. This whole complicated process may also be described as coping with the world by developing the powers and the integration of the ego; for all the skills on which the philobatic conquest of objects and of the world are based are functions of the integrated ego.

The ocnophil's regression by magic—i.e. by imagining the harmony—is also a primitive adaptation: equally acceptance and denial of the fact of separate existence, but he deals with it by primitive means which do not enable him to regress to the desired situation, except in fantasy. Though philobatic progression for the sake of regression demands the acquisition of a consummate skill, it enables one to regress to this early state of harmonious identity, not only in fantasy but also, to a great extent, in reality.

From another point of view the ocnophil deals with a traumatic situation by autoplastic means, i.e. he changes himself; instead of being held, he holds. Later a further step of autoplastic adaptation leads him to introject the object in order to prevent the ever-threatening danger of being dropped. In a way the philobat starts also with autoplastic adaptation, he changes himself while acquiring his skill, but then proceeds to use it for changing the world, in particular some of his objects, into co-operative partners. Thus he makes this important step from autoplastic to alloplastic adaptation.

Ocnophilia can be considered as a fixation to the first reaction provoked by a major trauma. The major trauma was the painful discovery of the independent existence of important objects. The first reaction is denial, the object is not independent: by clinging the ocnophil can reassure himself that he and his object are still one, inseparable. Thus, he copes with the world by developing his ability to enter into, and maintain, intimate object-relationships—a task of only secondary importance to a philobat.

The philobat suffered the same trauma, but the skill which he was able to acquire enabled him to re-create to some extent the destroyed harmony between his world and himself. The price he has to pay seems to be a never-ending repetition of the original trauma, a kind of traumatic neurosis. In order to regain the illusion of the friendly expanses, to experience the thrill, he has to leave the zone of safety and expose himself to hazards representing the original trauma. As we know, in pathological cases, especially in the age of puberty and adolescence, these hazards may be unrealistically severe. 'Thrill' admirably describes this queer integration of competing tendencies. Its original meaning, as we saw in Chapter IV, was to pierce something, causing a high-pitched noise—a mixture of pleasure and pain, both of high intensity.

I wish to repeat here, as I have already said in Chapter V, that the two words ocnophilia and philobatism were intentionally chosen so that both should contain the root 'love', thus stressing that they are not true opposites. To my mind they are both secondary states, developing out of the archaic phase of primary love as reactions to the traumatic discovery of the separate existence of objects. As they are both derivatives of the state of primary love, it is fitting that their names should bear witness to their origin.

It is equally true that both the ocnophil and the philobat are essentially ambivalent to their objects. The ocnophil is always suspicious, mistrusting, critical; the philobat always superior, condescending. Both of them are in constant danger —as perhaps all adult mankind is—of marring or even destroying their relation to their love objects by exactly the same methods by which they gained their favour: the ocnophil by the use of too much dependent clinging, the philobat by the use of too much superior skill. From this angle it would have been equally correct to describe these two attitudes by words denoting hatred. Apart from personal predilections, I have decided on love in order to express—in agreement with K. Abraham and S. Ferenczi—my firm belief in the existence of the primary pre-ambivalent state, which I prefer to call primary love.

By using the same root for my new technical terms, I also wanted to avoid some of the mistakes that we could not help making with regard to sadism and masochism. These two were at first regarded as truly antithetical—one the negative of the other, one perhaps more akin to love, or at least to health, than the other. Nowadays it has become gradually accepted that all these were false problems, due only to preconceived ideas, and having hardly any connection with clinical reality. Keeping at safe distance from the vexed problem of primary sadism and masochism, we may all agree that both sadism and masochism as observed in adults, and in fact in children of the verbal period, are neither antithetical nor primary. They are secondary, i.e. reactions to frustrations, their usual clinical appearance is as a mixture of the two, and they always have a long history in the individual's past. In the same way as with regard to sadism and masochism, it would be a nonsensical question to ask which of the two attitudes, philobatism or ocnophilia, is healthy.

To be more specific, which is healthier: to hold on anxiously to one's love objects in abject fear that they may change as soon as one loses touch with them or, on the contrary, to leave them time and again, confident that one will always be able to find new ones, or even that when returning to the old ones at one's whim one will find them unchanged in their affection? The answer clearly is: both these attitudes are more or less pathological. Health is obviously not dependent on the ingredients, but on their proper combination in suitable proportions.

To repeat: both ocnophilia and philobatism are chronologically secondary to the state of primary love, both imply an ambivalent attitude to objects, and both types use denial to rid their mind of certain unacceptable aspects of reality. They are ingredients only to be used in various proportions by the mind when building up its habitual patterns and methods for dealing with the problems created by the world of objects.

And lastly, I have deliberately used mainly the philobatic and ocnophilic attitudes to physical reality in my arguments. This was done for the sake of simplicity. Our vocabulary is such that it can more easily, and above all more unequivocally, describe external physical situations as compared with internal, mental situations. I would add here that everything said about the philobatic sportsman, athlete, or acrobat with regard to his body and the physical dangers of the external world should be understood as comprising the attitudes of philobatic thinkers, scientists, artists, with regard to their minds and the internal dangers of the psychological world. *Mutatis mutandis,* whatever we have found about the ocnophil's need for proximity and for constantly remaining in contact with his object should be held to include ocnophilic scientists, thinkers, artists, with regard to their internal world.

XI

REGRESSION IN THE
ANALYTIC SITUATION

In the previous chapter we found that the individual may
have three forms of primitive relation to the world around
him. The first of them, primary love, is represented by the
structureless friendly expanses. This harmonious relation is
but short-lived, the traumatic discovery that vitally important parts of it are both independent and inscrutable creates
a structure, and from then the world will consist of firm and
resistant objects and of spaces separating them. The individual's response to this trauma is, as we have seen, a complicated mixture of ocnophilia and philobatism.

At the beginning of Chapter VIII I pointed out that there
are possibly two spheres in which these three states of very
primitive object relationships may be observed and studied.
One is very early childhood, and the other highly regressed
patients in the analytic situation. I there discussed at some
length why it is so difficult to obtain reliable data about these
states. First, there is the intense dependence of the baby or
patient on us observers. This dependence is an essential
quality of the relationship, and forces us to become participants and partners in a highly emotionally charged situation.
Second, most of the experiences met in these situations belong
to pre-verbal—infantile or regressed—states, and it is we
who have to render them into words; thus we have to act
also as interpreter-informers and translators. And lastly, we
are inevitably also teachers and educators; both the baby and
the regressed patient have to learn from us how to express
themselves so as to be understood, first by us, then by themselves, and ultimately by their fellow-men. It is in this aspect
that the regressed patient offers fewer complications than the

young baby. Although in his regressed state he is beyond the world of words, he can come back from it and—although with great difficulty and with considerable help from us— can tell us something of what happened to him *in his own words*. It is perhaps this fact that could explain why practically all psycho-analytic discoveries have been made during analysis of adult patients, a few important ones during analysis of children who could already speak, but not one to my knowledge by direct observation of babies.

After this recapitulation let us now see how these three states—the undisturbed harmony of primary love, the post-traumatic ocnophilia, and philobatism—appear in our every-day clinical experience.

In quite a number of my analyses there occurs a period in which the patient feels a very strong urge or need to get up from the couch. Some patients are content to sit up, others want to stand—more often than not in a safe corner of the room farthest from my chair—and yet others have to walk about. Obviously this 'acting out' is overdetermined. One important factor is fear, forcing the patient away from the analyst; another defiance, 'not taking things lying down'; a third, curiosity; a fourth, naughtily testing out the analyst's tolerance, and so on. But there is also the factor that takes the patient away from a hazardous object, his analyst, and opens up for him expanses which, though not entirely friendly, are still felt to be less dangerous or less exciting than the proximity of the analyst. It is remarkable that no matter how defiant or how naughty, how frightened or agitated, the patient may have been, it has hardly ever happened in my whole experience that he has touched, or collided with, any object in my room. It is fair to say that in many respects these episodes are reminiscent of the philobatic states we have described. They are structured definitely on the pattern of the three-act drama, i.e. they start and end in the security of the couch, while the middle act never lacks the quality of fear and, above all, of thrill. Objects are skilfully and carefully avoided, while constant watch is kept on them, especially on the most hazardous object, the analyst. Although often the whole episode may impress one as an acute outbreak of fear, suspicion, and hostility, this is only part of the truth. This kind of philobatic acting out, if correctly recognised and handled by the analyst, reveals itself almost always as an important experience, a piece of working through, leading towards a better mutual understanding between patient and analyst. The establishment of this better understanding mainly depends upon whether or not the analyst can achieve a change in the patient's fantasy from a hazardous object into part of the friendly expanses which need no longer be defied or watched with suspicion. (See also Chapter XIII, Section 4.)

With quite a number of patients, though by no means all, one can observe a characteristic sequence of events during their treatment. A number of them start analysis with their eyes open, interested in and intently, almost anxiously, watching the objects around them in the consulting-room. It is only very gradually that they discover the possibility of closing their eyes, detaching their ocnophilic clinging attention from the objects of the external world, and turning to the events in their own mind. Of course a good many various anxieties of the ocnophilic type have had to be worked through to make this discovery possible.

When finally settled in this second phase, these patients feel as if they were wrapped up in some cosy, warm, structureless darkness which envelops them and protects them from the unsympathetic and unfriendly external world. To open their eyes in this state means to destroy the friendly darkness and to expose themselves to the unsympathetic, indifferent, or possibly hostile external world of separate objects.

It is only after long and intensive work on this second level that they can open their eyes again and look round in the world which is then no longer hostile, the objects of which need not be watched with suspicious attention. This sequence may also be described in a somewhat different way, as follows: (1) the patient feeling the need to fight for a place for himself in the world and being afraid of somebody or something pushing him out of it and not allowing him to have his place in peace; (2) withdrawing into a structureless and safe corner but not daring to move out of it; and (3) discovering, or perhaps only rediscovering, the possibility of finding friendly expanses in the world, no matter where his fate may lead him.

More or less parallel with these events another sequence occurs. This is the patient's changing relation in his fantasy to the couch offered him by his analyst. In the beginning the patient so to speak floats above the couch, hardly touching it; he lies rigidly, usually on his back, with his hands safely tucked away, either clenched or in his pockets, obviously avoiding any close contact with contaminated untrustworthy objects. In this state the couch is experienced and described as a horrid, dirty, god-forsaken thing.

Then the attitude of mistrust and avoidance gradually changes into a frightened ocnophilic clinging to the couch, burying himself in it, even holding fast to it, lest the couch, the world, the analyst, should turn out to be unreliable, and even drop him. In this period the patient usually finds it very difficult to end the session, as this means relinquishing the safety of his ocnophilic relation to the couch and being compelled to face the horrid, cold, empty spaces between the couch and his next possible object, e.g. the door.

Usually it is in this stage, after the ocnophilic anxiety has somewhat abated, that it happens that the couch changes into an exciting place, inviting the patient to undertake adventurous philobatic journeys by means of free associations. These hazardous adventures are made possible, however, only because the kind, cuddling safety represented by the couch is always there, near at hand, should the adventure turn out to be too exciting or even frightening.

This, then, gradually leads to a more relaxed atmosphere,

when the couch so to speak holds the patient safely. There is is no more need to cling, to hold fast; the patient entrusts the couch with his whole weight, in fairly safe confidence that it will be there, that it will be strong enough to hold him. In this period the patient usually allows himself some relaxation of posture, turns on his side, curls up, asks for and uses a rug, etc. The ending of the session in this period, although not very pleasant, can usually be tolerated in the confidence that the couch and the analyst will be there waiting for him at the coming session.

It is only in the very last phases of the treatment that the interchange between these states becomes easy and painless, although not by a long way emotionless. The patient can shut his eyes and envelop himself in his protective, cosy, structureless darkness, or open his eyes and find friendly expanses around him; he can allow the couch to carry his weight, and at the end of the session, so to speak, put his weight back on his own shoulders and carry it away with him—without great joy, but without bitter resentment.

There are a number of similarities between this development and that of the baby. At least in our civilisation the baby starts his existence—like our patients—mostly lying on his back. It is only after some weeks that he can lift his head, that he can focus his eyes and see objects properly; still later that he can turn on his side, and then on his tummy; and later still that he can pick himself up to crawl and then to walk away. Is this mere coincidence, of no importance at all, or ought we not to see in this parallel another example of the repetition compulsion? If the latter proposition is acceptable, I wish to stress that in this case the repetition involves both the patient and his analyst. When we start the treatment we offer a set-up to our patients which in almost every case induces them to adopt a babyish posture.

Yet another important subjective experience of the same period is what patients describe as 'sinking'. This feeling quite often precedes the regressive states described above.

Another equally favourite description is 'merging into' or 'submerging into' this state. German patients use the cognate word 'versinken' to describe this experience. The aspect which is most important for my train of thought is that the something into which, after overcoming his anxieties, the patient sinks or merges, is structureless, friendly, and existence in it is, in a way, simpler and easier, less complicated than everyday adult existence.

While patients get nearer in their regression to the states reminiscent of the primary object relationship, it quite often happens—in my practice—that, either angrily or good-humouredly, they wish the analyst would go to hell as he is felt to be too noisy; although it is true that his interpretations are correct and even helpful in clarifying the situation, they are not worth the bother. One patient, for instance, said: 'Balls to all your correct interpretations!'

All this, however, applies only to that part of the analyst's work that presupposes a somewhat adult attitude and expects rather adult responses from the patient. Interpretations, although highly important, certainly belong to this class. In contrast to the 'noisy' interpretations, the room itself, and especially the couch, the cushions, the rug, all of which are supplied by the analyst, remain all the time highly acceptable and welcome to the patient.

Usually at this stage the patient is also perturbed by the idea that he might hurt the analyst by wishing he would go to hell. In fact, it needs only very little work to discover that this wish means merely that the analyst should keep quiet and should not demand attention from his patient. On the other hand, it is most important that the analyst should be there, should stay with his patient, should not only do so but should enable the patient to remain aware all the time that the analyst is there for him. This must not amount, however, in any way to a demand that the patient should understand the analyst's interpretations and remain in active communication with him. What the patient wishes for are just slight signs, definitely undemanding signs, not even soliciting from him any attention or response, signs showing that the analyst is there with his patient. To quote an example: One patient when in this state asked me not to speak, to keep quiet, but occasionally to move a little, for instance to make my chair creak gently or let my breathing become somewhat audible, etc. But I was not allowed to use any words because they demanded to be understood, which meant coming out of this regressed state into the adult world of words.

Of course this transference-relation is over-determined, and all the determinants have to be interpreted in time and then worked through. One determinant is the ocnophilic fear of being abandoned or dropped by the object, and all the requests are, so to speak, for reassurance that this has not happened and will not happen. Another determinant may be the fear of having destroyed or damaged the object, in which case the requests are for reassurance that this is not the case, that the object—the analyst—is still whole and alive, is able to speak to and to understand his patient. A third possible determinant, and in my opinion the most important one, is that the analyst should become part and parcel of the patient's world, i.e. should assume the qualities of a primary object in complete harmony with him. In other words, the analyst should not be an entity in his own right, with his own ideas, clever suggestions, and profound interpretations, in fact not a separate sharply contoured object at all; but should merge as completely as possible into the 'friendly expanses' surrounding the patient.

Before leaving this topic I wish to mention one more subject which has many points of contact with the phenomena discussed in this chapter. This is the very vexed question of silence. The silent patient is of course one of the great problems of analytic technique, a problem for which I cannot offer any general solution. My only aim here is to point out its possible regressive nature.

I cannot give diagnostic criteria for discriminating, but I

think we all agree that silence in the analytic situation may have two meanings. One is a frightening experience of a horrible emptiness, full of suspicion, hostility, rejection, and aggressiveness; a silence which blocks progress and is on the whole barren. Silence can also be a tranquil, quiet experience of harmony, an atmosphere of confidence, acceptance, peace; a period of tranquil growth, of integration. It is most important for the analyst to recognise which of these two types of silence he has to deal with. This task is not made easier by the fact that quite often, although far from always, the patient's silence is a mixture of the two antithetical attitudes. Moreover, silence may have just the opposite meaning for the patient to what it subjectively has for his analyst. Obviously the danger is always present that the analyst's interpretations might be conditioned also by his subjective reactions or by his theoretical expectations. In any case, the parallel between these two types of silence and between the horrid empty spaces and the friendly expanses, respectively, is striking.

It is not only in the analytic situation that we meet these two opposite attitudes towards silence. In everyday life we meet people who adore silence, seek for solitude, and need it; and other people who hate silence, are only happy in noisy places, in crowded pubs, and, when coming home, the first thing they inevitably must do is to turn on the wireless.

In music, too, the pause—i.e. silence—has these two opposite effects. Depending on how it was arrived at, the effect of a pause, of silence, may be most peaceful, soothing, and calming, or on the contrary exceedingly tense and exciting or depressing. I think it is fair to say that silence can be as tense, frightening, and stimulating, or as tranquil or peaceful, as any tone, harmony, chord, or melody.

This antithetical nature of the effect of silence strongly suggests that it can mobilise in us powerful and very primitive energies, which again leads us back to my theory of primary object relationship.

98

Of course the primitive emotional attitudes just described do not occur during every analytic treatment, either in pure forms or in a regulated, easily observable sequence. What one gets to observe is a varying mixture, although, according to the particular complex and its concomitant anxieties that are being worked through, usually the situation is coloured chiefly by one attitude or the other. Moreover, the more intense the working through is, the more rarely does one find that only one attitude determines the whole atmosphere. On the other hand, after a successful piece of analytic work— e.g. towards the end of a particular working-through period —the situation usually becomes simpler and the main determinant more easily discernible. If, then, these successive winding-up attitudes are taken together during a longish stretch of analysis, in most cases a sequence emerges roughly corresponding to the description given in this chapter. I am fully aware how vague and uncertain my description is. This, however, cannot be remedied except by considerably more experience.

I would like to end this chapter with a personal note. It was in 1932, at the Wiesbaden Congress, that I first described the regressive states just mentioned, and stressed their great importance for analytic technique and theory.[1] Even then I was already deeply impressed by the sincerity and elementary nature of—what I would now call—the patient's ocnophilic needs. For some time I thought that these constituted an essential part of the earliest object relationship which I called primary love. It is only during the last few years that I have been able to disentangle the various elements reappearing in these regressed states, and to recognise their mutual chronological and dynamic relations as described in this book.

The most important difference between my earlier and my present views is as follows. I thought that the need to be

---

[1] See 'New Beginning' in the author's *Primary Love and Psycho-Analytic Technique*.

near to the analyst, to touch or to cling to him, was one of the most characteristic features of primary love. Now I realise that the need to cling is a reaction to a trauma, an expression of, and a defence against, the fear of being dropped or abandoned. It is therefore a secondary phenomenon only, its aim being the restoration by proximity and touch of the original subject-object identity. This identity, expressed by the identity of wishes and interests between subject and object, is what I call primary object relation or primary love.

All regressive states, not only those just described, are attempts at approaching the state of primary love. Why these regressed states occur during analytic treatment, what their therapeutic value is, and what role they play in the analytic process will be discussed in my forthcoming book: *The Three Areas of the Mind*. To conclude this part of my book I wish to say something about the analyst's responses and reactions to these states, i.e. about his technique with regard to a regressed patient.

XII

THE OCNOPHILIC AND PHILOBATIC BIAS OF OUR THEORY AND TECHNIQUE

OBVIOUSLY these states of regression can be reached only if patient and analyst tacitly or even explicitly agree that they should be reached. Certain analysts view regressions of this kind with suspicion, call them acting out, and interpret any move towards them as the patient's attempt to escape from the analytic work, especially from the agreed form of communication, viz. more or less continuous free associations by the patient, punctuated by appropriate interpretations by the analyst. It is understandable that in such an atmosphere this kind of tranquil unexcited regression does not occur, i.e. the analytic work is carried out more or less entirely in those layers of the mind which are accessible to words. Another group of analysts, less strict in their approach, may tolerate regressions of this kind but, perhaps unwittingly, force the patient out of them by their otherwise correct interpretations, for the acceptance and the understanding of their interpretations demands much more maturity from the patient than this state of regression can afford. Although regression may be reached for short moments, it cannot be maintained by the patient, and perhaps still less recognised by the analyst. This kind of analytic work is also kept mainly on the verbal level, allowing glimpses into the tranquil, unexcited pre-verbal states, but not permitting the patient to sink into them for any length of time.

A further important consequence of either of these two analytic atmospheres is a possible bias of our theory. Analysts working more or less according to the two methods just described will necessarily come to the conclusion that separate and particular objects are all-important for the human mind. Their everyday experiences will force upon their minds a theory of object relations which will be built on the model of ocnophilia. The danger of this is in any case great, since the psycho-analytic situation is built on exactly this pattern. In our traditional, well-proven setting the patient—as a rule— is lying on his back, a position which inevitably changes his actual picture of the world. Another important consequence of the traditional analytic set-up is that this new world inevitably entails that during the sessions the patient cannot see his most important object, his analyst, at all, and certainly not in 'proper proportion', in 'true perspective'. This is a change of paramount importance which contributes considerably to activating a regressive process. A further important factor is that henceforth he has to maintain relationship with an objective, in many respects indifferent, and, above all, independent, object—his analyst—of necessity allowing the patient at best only part satisfactions, which conversely means that he must equally of necessity force the patient to accept the state of part frustration as an intrinsic quality of reality.

Moreover, our present-day technique strongly advocates interpreting everything that happens in the analytic sessions also, or even primarily, in terms of transference, i.e. of object relationship. This otherwise justified and correct procedure leads to some unforeseen side results. One of these is that thereby the analyst, willy-nilly, must offer himself incessantly as an object to his patient, almost demanding to be clung to, and consistently interpreting anything contrary to clinging as an attempt at escaping from proper analytic work. Further unforeseen results of this procedure are: that we have developed a highly ocnophilic theory of object-relationships founded mainly on relationships to part-objects, and that we have made great advances in developing a theory of frustration and of ambivalence. An unforeseen and largely unrecognised consequence of this one-sided development is that the relations to whole objects and the phenomena of proper gratifications have been less well studied, and our theories about them are poor and scanty in comparison to those about relations to part-objects and about ambivalence and frustration.

As this proposition—viz. that our theory may have an ocnophilic bias—is important for my argument, I would like to enlarge upon it. In some of these regressed states the patient's main aim may be to get away, to free himself, from his oppressive objects. True, his objects are most important to him; he clings to them, he depends on them for his security, for his libidinous satisfactions and pleasures, for his mental balance. But as his neurosis proves, he has to pay a very heavy price for what he gets from them. Perhaps an important part of this price is the anxiety which he experiences whenever he tries to do away with them. Now, at long last, with the help of his analyst, he has reached the stage in which he dimly becomes aware of, and can even give faint expression to, his wish for freedom. Freedom according to my ideas means the rediscovery of the friendly expanses of the philobatic world demanding the possession of adult skills, and behind it the world of primary love which holds one safely without making any further demands on one. To avoid a possible misunderstanding, I would emphasise that this rediscovery does not mean an absolute giving up of all objects. On the contrary, it means only the giving up of desperate clinging, and acquiring the ability—the skill—to stand alone, at a distance from the objects, in order to get them in 'true perspective', to see them in 'proper proportions'.

If instead of allowing and merely witnessing this process of rediscovery, the analyst interferes with it by his otherwise correct interpretations, he may considerably restrict the patient's development towards freedom. What will probably happen is that the patient will be induced to introject the idealised image of his analyst,[1] i.e. to exchange one set of ocnophilic

---

[1] Cf. my paper 'Training Analysis and Analytic Training', *Int. J. Psycho-Anal.* (1954), **35**.

internal objects for another. Admittedly, this may be a good bargain for him, since the new set is far better adapted to reality, less restricting and less frightening than the old used to be. Henceforth he will be able to make good use of his analyst's skill, appropriated and introjected during the treatment, but it is questionable whether he will ever be able to give up his clinging, to stand on his own feet and see with his own eyes. As we have seen, the ocnophil must cling because in his fantasy it is he who is held as safely, as firmly as he can cling to his object, either externally or internally.

The analyst who does not take into account either in his theoretical views or in his technique the world of primary love and of the friendly expanses, of course will find only confirmation for his own ocnophilic ideas in his practice. Moreover, whenever he sees moves in his patient towards regression into those friendly expanses, he will consistently interpret them as attempts at escaping from proper analytic work, viz. at getting rid of or destroying the analyst. These interpretations will be correct as far as they go; they stress one determinant of an overdetermined situation and prevent the recognition of all the others.

Moreover, standing on one's own, venturing into unknown lands, is, as a rule, frightening, especially for one with ocnophilic tendencies. It is much safer to allow one's analyst to 'take one by the hand', especially in moments when one has to face an anxious situation. This kind of dependent ocnophilic attitude is further reinforced by the analyst's correct interpretations that the patient wishes to get rid of him, to destroy him who has been so kind, understanding, sharp-witted, and ever-helpful. If consistently repeated, the never fully absent guilt feelings, reinforced by this kind of interpretation, cannot fail to bring the patient round out of his attempts to regress into the world of friendly expanses, to an ocnophilic attitude towards his analyst. The result will be a convincing confirmation of a theory with a strong ocnophilic bias; that is, a theory based prominently on the study of ambivalent relations to part objects, and embodying a great amount of unsatisfiable anger and rage on the one hand, and profound guilt feelings and abject contrition on the other.

Despite this general tendency of analysis towards creating or, at any rate, reinforcing ocnophilic attitudes in our patients, according to published material it happens surprisingly often that patients use the imagery of philobatism when describing their subjective experiences at the end of their treatment. Time and again we read phrases such as: the world has opened up for him, at long last he can stand on his feet, his eyes are sweeping new horizons, at the end of a long, dark tunnel he can see the light, and so on; all variations on the same theme. To my mind they all originate from a philobatic imagery. This finding is a serious warning that my criticism, that our present technique has a strong ocnophilic bias, may be unjust and incomplete, inasmuch as there must be other strong forces also at work. This latter is doubtless true, but before discussing these other forces let us see what the snags of a possibly 'philobatic' technique are.

If I am right, a technique with a philobatic bias would use interpretations, especially *vis-à-vis* a regressed patient, rather sparingly. The analyst will be constantly watching whether he should accept the role of a separate object, looking at his regressed patient from a safe distance and giving, from his detached, objective point of view, interpretations couched in words which demand to be understood; or whether he should merge into the friendly expanses, not demanding anything, just remaining alive and available for his patient should any need arise. The rationale of this technique is that by his quiet undemanding and unexacting attitude the analyst will avoid the danger of forcing his patient to introject his idealised image. Instead, he hopes the patient will have the possibility of approaching the original traumatic situation as he chooses, either by associations or by regression, working through the anxieties barring his way, and then—without much interference by his analyst—he may eventually develop the requisite personal skills necessary for adult life.

This is a beautifully idealised picture, I know. So let us discuss the dangers inherent in it. The greatest danger, to my mind, is that this technique may leave too much to the patient, forcing on him too much independence too early; this, then, in the same way as the ocnophilic technique may lead to introjecting the aggressor, in this case the philobatic analyst as a demanding figure, exacting heroic standards from his poor patients. I would emphasise that consistent interpretations of the anxieties caused by the prospect of becoming independent might be of very little help, as they might be felt by the patient as a gentle but incessant force, pressing him to accept and adopt the philobatic, heroic standards. *Gutta cavat lapidem, non vi sed saepe cadendo* is thus a memento equally to be borne in mind for the ocnophilic and the philobatic technique. Certainly no one of us wants to wear down or 'hollow out' our patients in order to fill the vacuum thus created by introjects.

From another angle one may say that being neurotic means lacking in some or in many respects the skills necessary for adult life. To the analyst desiring to help his patient to acquire or develop these skills there are at least two possibilities open—neither of them without dangers. One is the ocnophilic method, 'taking the patient by the hand', i.e. interpreting consistently why he makes some moves and avoids others. The inherent risk is that the patient might be induced to introject his idealised analyst as a benevolent, permissive, protective figure, and from then on his freedom will be limited to what his idealised internal object will prescribe and tolerate. The other is the philobatic method, offering friendly expanses to the patient and 'quietly witnessing' his progress, being always there, always available, but interfering with him as little as possible. The inherent risk is that the patient might experience his analyst's expectant 'witnessing' attitude as an unconditional demand and introject him as an exacting figure, expecting heroic standards from him. I have no generally valid technical prescription to offer against this apparently ubiquitous danger of identification with the aggressor. My aim was to call attention to these hazards inherent perhaps in every kind of consistent analytic technique.

The result of this kind of introjection—no matter whether it was forced upon the patient by ocnophilic or philobatic techniques—is the acquisition of an efficient shell.[1] This shell has a double function. It supplies the individual with various skills necessary for life, but at the same time it restricts his possibilities of experiencing either love or hatred, either joy or misery. Life will reach him only with such intensity and in such form as his shell allows. One gets the impression that the ocnophil's objects are in a way parts of his shell, hence his highly ambivalent feelings towards them. On the other hand, the philobat's adventures while courting real dangers in search of thrills may be rebellious attempts to crack by realistic fears the efficient shell in order to get in touch with his real self hidden behind it. Neither of these states allows much freedom to feel or indeed to live; their development should be watched and avoided, in education as well as during analytic treatment.

This is easier said than done. What we need above all is more knowledge about the patient's imperative need to regress and the meaning of the various ways that patients use during regression. As I have tried to show in the previous chapter, the regressions in the analytic situation—if they are allowed to develop—constitute a mixture of ocnophilic and philobatic tendencies, and behind them what I call the world of primary love.

I hope my ideas may contribute something towards under-

---

[1] S. Ferenczi, *Notes and Fragments, passim.* Reprinted in *Final Contributions.* London: Hogarth Press, 1955. Originally written in 1931–2. D. W. Winnicott: 'Pediatrics and Psychiatry', in *Brit. J. Med. Psych.* (1948), **21**, 229.

standing our patients in their regressed states. However, I am fully aware that the main problems remain unsolved: Why is it that the need to regress is much stronger in some patients than in others? What are the processes that determine the depth of the regression in each case, that bring about its end and enable the patient to emerge from it a better man in some cases, and why in other cases, despite every effort, do we fail? A knowledge of these factors may be the basis of a reliable differential diagnosis, so badly needed in this field. We still know all too little.

PART III

Appendix

XIII

NOTES ON SOME KINDRED TOPICS

(1) *Data on the History of Physical Thrills*

As mentioned in Chapter II, for many centuries the normal pattern was that professionals performed various acts causing thrills in spectators. A change which turned spectators in increasing numbers into actors started slowly, almost imperceptibly, about the middle of the nineteenth century—as, for instance, the beginnings of amateur alpinism—and has been gathering momentum ever since. The history of this change would certainly be a most rewarding study for a social psychologist. All I can do here is to record some data regarding it.

According to the *Shorter Oxford Dictionary* 'swing' is an old Teutonic word first recorded in the intransitive sense in 1528. 'Roundabout', in the meaning of merry-go-round, is first found in 1484, and was freely used already by Shakespeare. The word 'merry-go-round' dates back to 1728, while 'switchback' is a recent arrival, appearing in the late 1880s. It is remarkable that the saying, 'What you lose on the swings you gain on the roundabouts', which sounds an old-established proverb, dates only from 1912.[1]

The first description in English literature of funfair swings, roundabouts, and the vertical wheel (*Riesenrad*) is by Peter Mundy. He saw them in Philippopolis (now Plovdiv in Bulgaria) in 1620. The swings were for both adults and children, but the roundabouts and wheels for children only. So it remained for quite a long time, as long as human effort supplied the motive power. Later ponies were harnessed to the wheels, then steam engines, and from about 1910 electricity also. The greater motive power allowed the use of

[1] *Oxford Dictionary of English Proverbs*, 2nd ed.

heavier structures, higher speeds, and offered enjoyment for adults also.[1]

I would like to add one more point which no study of this field can afford to neglect. The professional acrobat must himself assess the risks he can and dare take, and himself devise methods of coping with them; in other words, he is the responsible man, the father figure, ambivalently admired by the spectator-children. Our philobatic contemporaries in funfairs entrust all this work and responsibility to the designers of the amusement machines, the craftsmen, and the licensing and supervising authorities. It is these unknown, unremembered, but reliably benevolent father-figures who devise the acceptable risks and the safe methods for coping with them; in fact, the funfair fan is a mere child in the guise of a hero. There is some difference between him and the sportsman. The high-speed driver, the flyer, the mountain-climber, the skier, the diver, takes a much greater share in assessing the dangers, is relying much more on his own resources. He is, however, almost always assisted and looked after by professionals, i.e. reliable father-figures, such as car mechanics, mountain guides, ski-ing instructors, coaches, and swimming-pool constructors. Still, despite these benevolent guardians the philobat exposes himself apparently unnecessarily to real dangers in his search for thrills. The problem is rather different in the case of the professional philobats who earn their living by accepting very serious risks. This difference is perhaps not of fundamental importance, as exemplified by the professional Tensing and the amateur Hillary reaching the summit of Everest together, on the same rope.

(2) *Sublimation and Art*

These two topics are closely related to each other as well as to the two attitudes discussed in this book. Although every

[1] All these data are taken from Thomas Murphy, 'The Evolution of the Amusement Machine', *Journal of the Royal Society of Arts*, **49**, No. 4855, 1951.

artistic creation and, for that matter, every sort of sublimation originates in the internal world, their aim is always to achieve a change in the external world; in other words, both art and sublimation are forms of alloplastic adaptation to objects. The fact that they belong to the borderland between the internal and the external worlds explains the queer sort of reality testing inherent in both. For the artist external reality is in many ways just a nuisance, highly annoying by its insistence, but otherwise only of secondary importance; whereas artistic creation means everything and is incomparably more important than the external world. In another respect, however, the artist resembles the philobat; for both of them testing of reality in their particular field is paramount. For the painter, the colour must be of just that hue and brilliance, the line must have exactly that kind of sweep, delicacy, or toughness, the contrast of colours and the harmony integrating them must be achieved on the canvas, i.e. in reality, exactly as he envisaged them in his creative fantasy. *Mutatis mutandis*, the same is true of all artists. For the dancer, the rhythm and the spatial relation of his movements; for the sculptor, the surface texture and the proportions of his carving; for the poet, the weight and cadence of his words; for the playwright, the exact timing of the dialogue, etc., must comply inexorably with the demands of his fantasy; that is, his achievement must be able to stand up to a searching reality testing. In the same way as the philobat, the artist too must keep up the standard of his performance by constant practice and never-relaxing self-criticism; any deviation from the right standard may lead to humiliating failure.

There is yet another important parallel. Although it is not known for certain what an empty canvas or a clean sheet of paper represents to the painter or to the poet, doubtless they are, before the creative process starts, an empty world which may mean either 'a horrid empty space', 'a friendly expanse', or 'a harmonious mix-up'. My guess is that the meaning varies with the artist's personality, and even in the same artist may vary with time. But whatever the artist's original attitude may be, this empty world will be filled by objects created into it, a process reminiscent of the discovery of objects discussed in Chapter VII. This change from a harmonious, friendly, exciting, or horrid emptiness into a world filled with objects (or with one object only) is an event of great importance and, as a rule, artists are aware of, and can even describe, what happens during it. Their description is not so seldom reminiscent of the philobatic three-act drama: the feeling of despair and fear, or excitement and exhilaration, when the creative process starts and the artist must leave—either voluntarily or forced by his internal processes—his security; the thrill or the apprehension experienced when entering the philobatic world, often feeling the deed as dangerous and heroic; and lastly, the satisfaction or restful tranquillity after having filled the void with objects. The objects created are of course the various characters in the novel or play, the people or objects represented on the canvas, the sculpture chiselled out of the block of marble, and so on.

As mentioned in Chapter VII, there is an interesting change of terminology—occurring, so far as I know, solely in the English language—which admirably describes this transitional nature of artistic creation: the real content of a work of art is never called its object but its subject-matter. This somehow conveys to us that although the work, which now exists in the external objective world as an object, a piece of matter, really belongs to the subjective world; yet in addition it has all the attributes of the non-aggressive primary world, where there is as yet no difference between subject and object, a world of harmonious mix-up, merging into the subject and holding it safely. The French language is not quite exact on this point. The subject-matter of an artistic creation is called simply 'le sujet', over-emphasising the importance of the subjective world and ignoring the fact that external physical matter is invariably and inseparably involved in any artistic activity. Apparently some analysts, though writing in English, prefer the French way of feeling and speaking about art.

Creating a safe and solid object is reassuring and satisfactory, and so is its counterpart: beholding it. Both of them mean that there can be things, beautiful and enjoyable, which seem to be almost inviolate, which may have existed before us and probably will continue to exist long after our death, which may be indeed *ære perennius*. Modern art, which tends to dissolve the objects and threatens to merge them once again back into their environment, undermines this reassuring experience.[1] The diminishing importance or even complete disappearance of objects must give rise to ocnophilic fears which may explain why certain people have such an inexplicable resistance to, and even disgust for, modern art, while others, more philobatically attuned, welcome it with open arms, occasionally without any criticism.

An interesting reaction against this dissolution of objects is surrealist art. If I understand the surrealists' intentions correctly, they reject most emphatically the idea that the artist must *represent* the objects of the world faithfully or in any other way; according to them the artist must *create* objects according to his internal needs and conceptions. It is almost as if the evolution of art had completed a full circle; the surrealist's objects are usually clearly delimited, sharply contoured, reminiscent of the first period of art described in my paper cited above.

As already described by Freud, all sublimations, and especially the form of sublimation called art, are a kind of deception, are underhand ways of getting back to real personal objects. All the achievements of the artist, his creations, etc., are in fact roundabout ways of conquering human objects—i.e. people—without admitting that this is

---

[1] Cf. 'Dissolution of Object Representation in Modern Art' (1952). Reprinted in *Problems of Human Pleasure and Behaviour, op. cit.*

his real aim. In order to save their self-esteem most artists pretend that their main aim is creation, and not the winning of applause, of consideration, of appreciation. In this way they remind us of the philobat, who performs his thrilling exploits to impress himself—and his public—but returns without publicity into the zone of safety, of objects.

(3) *The Healing Power of Pure Water and Air*

Perhaps the symbolic significance of water and air as representatives of the friendly expanses may explain a number of curious age-old therapeutic applications which, though empirically found effective in a surprisingly varied number of illnesses, have never been really understood and still less scientifically validated.

One is the belief in the healing power of certain waters which in German, characteristically, are called 'Heilwässer'. The English language has no specific word for them and calls them simply 'waters'. An important feature is that, on the whole, the same water is used both for bathing and for drinking. In recent years they have been also used for a third purpose—colonic lavage. Pharmacology has tried, ever since the introduction of scientific methods, to discover what the healing power in these waters might be; at various times it has been thought to be due to their temperature, their salt content, then, with the advent of the ion theory, to their various cations and anions or to their particular combinations, to their acidity or alkalinity, then to their radio-active contents—without any success. The only result of this period of highly exact scientific analysis is that all mineral waters sold must bear a label stating their mineral contents, which everybody by now knows to be more or less irrelevant. This has gone to the extent of a number of them bearing the magnificent description 'oligo-mineral water', which literally means that they are practically free from anything, they are 'pure' water.

Nevertheless, although greatly diminished, the belief still

prevails that taking the baths or drinking the waters is an efficient therapeutic procedure in a great number of diseases. According to my ideas, the therapeutic effect is in the regressive fantasies surrounding existence in water, or taking water in, provided always that the water is pure, i.e. free from hazardous objects.

Something similar happened with our beliefs in the healing power of pure air. Doctors have always recommended and still recommend a change of air, but nowadays nobody takes it literally, it is understood metaphorically only. In Victorian times doctors still prescribed—of course only for wealthy patients—that so many bottles of alpine or sea air should be opened in the bedrooms at night. With the air the same thing happened as with the waters. Chemical or physical analysis of the sea or alpine air could reveal no therapeutic agent, although at various periods various factors were claimed, the two that still survive being ozone and ultra-violet rays. Though we know now for certain that none of these claims could be validated, we know equally well that a 'change of air' is in many cases highly beneficial. As the air recommended must be thought to be 'pure', according to my ideas its healing power is based on the same mechanism as in the case of the waters.

In both cases the alleged healing power is limited closely to purity. Purity, translated into my ideas, means complete absence of suspicious and hazardous objects, i.e. as close an approximation to the 'harmonious mix-up' or 'friendly expanses' as is physically possible.

(4) *The Psychology of Motility*

As yet, it has not been discussed why the method in practically all the phenomena described as progression for the sake of regression (see Chapters X and XI) takes the form of movement. When looking up the literature about it, I was surprised to find how little is known about the psychology of movement. What we know about it are its disturbances, such as its becoming over-cathected by some fantasy of an erotic nature, mostly belonging to the period of the Oedipal incest. These fantasies are then subjected to very severe repression, and when they unconsciously cathect any form of activity, this becomes a symbolical expression of the incestuous wish and has to be inhibited.

Apart from this, the literature contains hardly any information. To quote one example of the many, sleepwalking—which is a fairly frequent disturbance in childhood or even in later years—is a practically untouched enigma for which no proper explanation has been proposed. This criticism applies equally to me, as even my present ideas do not contribute anything to its understanding. So we are thrown back on to an often quoted idea of Freud's in his book *Beyond the Pleasure Principle*. There he mentioned the play of a small boy, just emerging from the pre-verbal period, who, according to Freud's idea, tried to cope with a traumatic situation, which he had to endure passively, by producing it intentionally and actively. According to Freud the trauma was that his mother, so important to him, had to leave him for long periods; expressed in my phraseology, the boy felt abandoned or dropped by his primary object. His reaction was to drop his favourite toy, and at the same time to acquire the skill for recovering it. This can be described, without any straining of a point, as progression for the sake of regression; moreover, the element of endless repetition which we found characteristic of philobatism is also present. If we accept this explanation we arrive at the conclusion that one, perhaps the most efficient, way of dealing with the consequences of a trauma is to produce it actively and intentionally, provided we can create circumstances in which we may feel certain that the skills we have acquired will be sufficient to prevent the recurrence of the shock caused by the original trauma.

Perhaps the endless repetition, reminiscent of traumatic neurosis, is an attempt at reassuring ourselves that our skill is definitely sufficient to undo any effect of a new trauma should it ever strike us again. The fact that the philobat must obtain this reassurance again and again suggests that he must have the thrills in order to keep his doubts about the reliability of his skills in check.

Returning now to Freud, it is rather humiliating to realise that in a few pages published in 1905[1] practically everything is contained that psycho-analysis has contributed to the psychology of voluntary motility, and that in more than fifty years since hardly anything new has been added to it.

Freud there described the exciting nature of both passive and active movement—in the form of being rocked and swinging on the one hand, romping, wrestling, getting wild on the other. He emphasised, too, what we should call today the forepleasure nature of these sensations, that is to say that they provide at one and the same time both sexual excitement and sexual gratification; in one way they are outlets for sexual excitation, in another they stimulate genital excitement and lead often either to masturbation or to various passionate sexual plays. He then adds that if the experiencing of pleasure is inhibited by repressions anxiety develops, and he gives as an example that of *Reisefieber*; in Chapter VIII I tried to discuss the possible reason why he used this symptom as an illustration.

It may be added that neither in the *Three Essays* nor anywhere else so far as I know does Freud mention any connection whatever between one's attitude towards movement, and one's object-relationships or one's relations to one's environment.

(5) *Water, Sand, and Words*

Over and above those mentioned in Chapter VII, there are further differences between what objects and substances mean to us. An object can be broken, injured, damaged, or destroyed, as every child very soon learns when playing with

[1] S. Freud, *Three Essays on Sexuality* (1905), Standard ed., Vol. VII, pp. 201–3.

his toys. A substance, a matter—such as water, sand, or in some respects even Plasticine—cannot be broken or damaged, cannot be destroyed. As substances do not resist or resist only little, all sorts of things can be done to them and with them that are absolutely impossible with objects. In contrast to objects one can enjoy them without the need for controlling one's own aggressiveness.

There are periods when every child is fascinated by water-taps, which, as if by magic, can produce a jet or can make it disappear. Moreover, although the jet is there and can be deflected or even stopped by the hand, as soon as the hand is removed the jet reappears as if nothing had happened. The same is true about turning off the tap and turning it on again. Almost in the same way as water, sand can be shaped, wetted, dried, a castle built from it destroyed and built up again, and so on in endless variations. It is obvious from the foregoing that neither sand nor water is a real object but a kind of precursor of the object.

Child-therapists respond to this difference roughly in two ways. One school of them maintains that no proper therapy can be carried out without offering the child sand and water. The other school rejects these two and offers only more or less hard and separate objects to the child, such as marbles, animals, cars, dolls, soldiers, building bricks, and so on. Plasticine, drawing, and painting constitute a transitional class. In view of the foregoing, it is to be expected that the responses elicited by the two extreme worlds created by the therapist will also differ somewhat; in particular the method which offers sand and water freely will possibly get as response smaller amounts of guilt feelings and inhibitions, and a freer release of aggressiveness; on the other hand, to offer only objects may activate in the child tendencies of preserving and reparation, and this leads him to realise his ambivalence conflicts and to face his depressive anxieties.

Words occupy a borderland position between these two worlds. On the one hand, they belong to the world of substances, they are indestructible, you cannot handle them, like water they run through your fingers. On the other hand, they are definitely limited with regard to time; one can easily decide where each word begins and ends. Despite their immaterial nature they seem to have some magic power that can influence the world of objects; if they are used in a proper way, things do happen. In this way they seem to belong to a somewhat later period of mental development; possibly they are post-depressive.

It would be a most interesting piece of research to find out the nature of pre-verbal symbols—such as images, pictures, movements—that denote or represent some object in the external world. We know something about the immense importance of magic gestures in psychology, in anthropology, and in folk-lore, in particular about their effect on the spectators or audience, but hardly anything about their effect on the magician-performer himself. The main significance of words is symbolical; that is, they denote or represent parts of the external world in a more or less unequivocal form. It is to be expected that gestures, movements, and other pre-verbal symbols will do something similar, only they will be more akin to the primary process; in contrast to words— which belong, on the whole, to the world of the secondary process—their meaning will not be settled firmly. Doubtless there will be found many transitional phenomena; one of them, called the cluster of associations surrounding each word, has been referred to on several occasions in this book.

(6) *The Three-act Drama in Sexuality*

In a way, the three-act drama that we discovered as the essential structure of all thrills is present also in all sexual pleasures; the usual pattern is that the individual is prompted —either by his own urges or by external stimulation—to abandon the safe zone of tranquil existence, expose himself more or less voluntarily to situations which inevitably increase the tension he has to bear, in the hope that his skills will enable him to enjoy these situations, release the tension by gratifying his urges, and that eventually he will be able to return unharmed to the safety of tranquil existence. This structure is obvious in genitality, but is also present in all forms of sexual experience. This similarity is the justification for calling sexual pleasures also sexual thrills.

A further important aspect of sexuality is its repetitive character, which has served as a basis for a number of analytic speculations about its nature; may I add one more to this number. If we assume that the repetition-compulsion in human sexuality received further impetus by the trauma caused by the discovery that our important objects have a life independent from us, then we understand why one aim of every form of sexual gratification is to restore, at least with one particular object, our beloved one, the harmonious mix-up that existed in the pre-object world; at the climax of pleasure one has the rapturous experience that, for that brief moment, there is complete harmony between oneself and the whole world.

Using these ideas, certain well-known sexual abnormalities may be recognised as over-determined. An added cause for impotence and frigidity may be the individual's inability to relax his hold on his object and start off on the hazardous exploits in the second act of our drama. He, or she, may enjoy greatly the first act, the tranquillity and the physical proximity, but not be able then to let himself go, as he might find himself alone without his object. A similar explanation will hold true for the—fairly frequent—fear or unwillingness to submit to the sensation of orgasm even a fraction of a second before one is absolutely sure that one's partner will be there too. Another abnormality connected with the fear of losing one's object is abject sexual bondage (*Hörigkeit*).

The philobatic disturbances and abnormalities represent the obverse of this picture. There are people who cannot tolerate any object—especially an independent object— assuming importance, and must either crush its independence or abandon it altogether; they are known as the Don Juan and Messalina types. It is possible that nymphomania belongs to the same group.

(7) *Pre-visual Material of Fantasy*

I have pointed out on several occasions in this book that the ocnophil does not, or even cannot, look because he must be as near as possible to his objects or must shut his eyes and turn his head away if danger threatens. On the other hand, the philobat can look because he is at a distance and does not turn his eyes away from the oncoming danger. It would be an intriguing study to investigate whether philobatism and the capacity for convergence—that is, the establishment of binocular vision—are connected with each other, and if so, how.

Fantasy—at any rate as far as we analysts are able to study it—is experienced in visual images, i.e. it may have a closer connection with philobatism than with ocnophilia. If we bear in mind that fantasies are mostly visual, then we are faced with the problem of finding out what the material is in which the ocnophil originally experiences his fantasies.

I think it is fair to assume that there must be fantasies already in the ocnophilic period. If so, they must be structured on the basis of ocnophilic experiences, since it is unlikely that ocnophils use visual imagery to the extent that it is used by philobats, we come to the conclusion that there must be some pre-visual material out of which ocnophilic fantasies are built. This pre-visual mental material probably consists of sensations of touch, of warmth, of smell, and taste; that is to say, rather indistinct but highly emotionally-charged sensations of what are called the lower senses.

On the basis of what we found about the three early pictures of the world—the harmonious mix-up of primary love, the horrid empty spaces of ocnophilia, and the friendly expanses of philobatism—it is possible to make some further assumptions. The pre-visual material for ocnophilic fantasies will be structured according to the pattern of the 'harmonious mix-up' or of the 'horrid empty spaces', possibly with sudden, almost traumatic, transitions from one to the other. Clinical experience seems to confirm this assumption; there are periods in every 'deep' analysis in which patients experience their environment, including their analyst, as being in complete harmony with them, and others in which they experience being alone, abandoned, in a God-forsaken, empty void. Moreover, these fantasies have hardly any visual element; they consist of sensations of touch, temperature, often accompanied by smells, occasionally by sensations of taste. This may be a promising field for research into the deeper layers of the mind.

XIV

DISTANCE IN SPACE AND TIME

by Enid Balint

In the previous chapters the philobat has been described as a person who finds pleasure in existing or moving about in what are to him friendly open spaces; who is not so much interested in leaving a place or arriving at another, as in the thrills and pleasures he experiences during his journey. These thrills are proportionate to his satisfaction in his skills, physical and mental, which enable him to make the journey. His pleasures therefore are partly in himself, in his own competence and power, and partly in the achievement which allows him to feel at one with objectless space. He is self-sufficient and fears no competitors for the favours of his objects, since he is not dependent on unobtainable objects.

The ocnophil is a person whose pleasure is found not in journeying from one place or object to another but in being in one place close to an object which he needs and values. He has no narcissistic pleasure in his mental or physical achievement; his satisfaction lies not in giving anything to his objects, but in getting something from them and being in close proximity to them.

The philobat finds satisfaction in his activity; he is really capable of journeying in the open spaces. The ocnophil, on the other hand, seems to have less satisfaction because even when clinging to his object he is never sure that it will not let him down. It may be said that the ocnophil has pleasure only in a negative way; that is to say, that he would have less pleasure or even displeasure if he were prevented from clinging; clinging is the best he can manage. He cannot have pride in himself, nor does he get real comfort from his objects.

APPENDIX

This description gives an idea of the relation the ocnophil and the philobat have to their own bodies and to the physical world outside them, but does not offer an adequate account of the psychological problems involved. What in fact does journeying from one place to another mean to the philobat, or clinging to an object to the ocnophil? To illustrate these two points, I will use material from the analyses of various patients.

One of them, whom I shall call A, reported a dream as follows: 'She was in the garden of a house; unpleasant food was being sold, which was in fact parts of human bodies. She then set out with the analyst on a tandem bicycle across a desert. Then followed a long description of this journey. There were carcasses of animals along the roadside. Finally an oasis was reached, but the patient was then made to carry a burden for the rest of the journey.' This dream was interpreted as a symbolic expression of the contrast between the patient's feelings about feeds and the time-span between feeds. She had no difficulty in journeying from one place to another and felt at home in the desert, but to her travelling *was* a desert. The oases—feeds—were felt to be slightly better than the desert, but still unsatisfactory and likely to lead to fresh burdens.

This dream, I would suggest, describes an extreme case of an inner world in which neither the journey nor the points of departure and arrival are satisfactory; there is no point in clinging to the oases—the feeds—nor is there much point in journeying on; yet the journey must be, and in fact can be, made.

Another patient, B, rather less ill than the former, throughout her analysis dealt with the passing of time as if it did not exist. She denied to herself that time did in fact pass, that changes and movements in her life did occur or, for that matter, that movements were necessary and inevitable; in her fantasy she imagined that she could, if only the analyst were good enough, remain always the same age and be looked after for the rest of her life. For her there should be no journeying from one place, age, or object, to another; everything should stand still, and she should be looked after, remaining the same age, and in the same place, for ever.

Neither of these patients was what might be called a 'mental' philobat, though the former, a fully-trained scientist, was a 'physical' philobat; she did, in fact, excel at horse-riding, enjoyed ski-ing, and was good at games. My feeling is that this patient acquired her competence in the various sports partly because she knew she would have to journey from one place to another, since no one place could be satisfactory to her. The other patient, who during the first year of life had some satisfactory periods with her mother, felt let down if she was ever left alone, and denied the existence of the passing of time; later in life she could not develop philobatic skills, and had even repressed her ocnophilic clinging, which only became manifest in her analysis. In consequence, she never had a clinging relationship with people in the external world; she had, in fact, a minimum of real objects in her life.

In my opinion the ideas developed in the previous chapters about the influence of distances in space should be extended to cover the influence of distances in time. Thus it could be said that philobats are people who have overcome at an early age the difficulty caused by the time-lag between one satisfaction and the next by transferring their enjoyment and love from the satisfactory moment itself to their ability to pass through the time between two satisfactions. The ocnophils, never having overcome the difficulty of the time between satisfactions, have come either to deny its existence or to flee from anything that is reminiscent of the early difficulty. In fact, I would suppose that the philobatic journey in space can be thought of as psychologically equivalent to the passage through time.

To illustrate this point I would like to quote some further clinical material. Two of my patients, C and D, had diffi-

APPENDIX

culties about time, and at first glance it looked as if these difficulties were of diametrically opposite character. One of them, C, the more ill of the two, could never be in time for anything. She had the compulsion to fill up her days with so many appointments that she could never finish one job without already being late for starting out on her journey to the next. It seemed as if everything that she was doing had to happen at the same time. I have the impression that the flat she lived in was similarly littered with objects that filled up every corner. The patient herself felt hopeless about ever being able to do anything in an orderly manner. Her profession demanded that she should travel from place to place, and this travelling gave her the greatest difficulty because she could not bear to think, still less to calculate, how long it would take her to get from one job to the next. She often made great efforts to estimate how much time she must allow for the journey, and then tried hard to convince me that in fact the journey would only take so long—although we both knew that the time allowed was unrealistic, since she was always and invariably late. She could not even read through a whole book, because the strain of having to acknowledge that there was a time factor in reading was too great; what she wanted was just to pick up a book and finish reading it in a flash.

For C time did not really exist, she could tolerate only the expectation of a series of objects, excitements, happenings, with no space or time between them. It was a long time before she could bear me to interrupt her during the analytic hour. She longed to have my interpretations and behaved as if she wanted nothing more than that I should tell her about things, give her advice, answer her questions, and so on, but in fact whenever I tried to speak it was with great difficulty that she could let me finish a sentence. What I said was never satisfactory enough, and she could not bear to wait to tell me something else which she then hoped would make my next intervention more satisfactory. With this patient apparently no excitement or gratification had ever been fully satisfactory, nevertheless she wanted them incessantly. In fact, she had wanted them so much that when they had come she could not bear to wait, for instance, to take in the food: she wanted to have had it without even the process of feeding coming between her and total satisfaction.

This leads me to another patient, D, who also found it difficult to spend time in travelling from one place to another, and had to take taxis in order to shorten the time needed for the journey. On the other hand, she could not bear to be late and found it impossible to keep people waiting for her. For her the idea that travelling from one place to another took any length of time was intolerable, and so it had to be cut down. Though she could enjoy satisfactions and excitement, or contacts with her objects, at times she spoilt her chances by making too great ocnophilic demands on her objects when she reached them.

Although these two patients could get satisfaction in a variety of ways—both were artistic—eating had a special meaning for them. They enjoyed the odd snack, the between-meals coffee, much more than the routine meals of the day. Symbolically stolen meals or satisfactions were always sought after but never enjoyed without guilt. Enjoyment of the cup of coffee or snack was usually marred because it had to be taken in a hurry, and they were afraid all the time that somebody might discover them having it, which would cause intense embarrassment. For them the odd meal meant having satisfactory periods on their own or being oblivious of time, which they were not able to enjoy.

My next example is a patient, E, who during one stage of her analysis said continually that she wished time would stand still. Her need was that she should be left alone, and that no demands should be made upon her, that she should not be expected to grow or perhaps even breathe during a process of timelessness. She did not need to cling to objects, she was in fact a mental philobat, but she preferred to have someone there when she was alone; that is, someone who made no demands on her and on whom she made no demands, except that the person should just remain quietly at hand. If any demands were made on her when she was merging into this kind of quiet timelessness, she was apt to get very angry and felt as if she had been assaulted. It appears that for her the most satisfactory period was not the time when she actually experienced gratification, but the time afterwards when she could dream about the gratification and felt at one with her environment.

This leads to another topic: the subjective experience of the duration of time. Many patients, E among them, felt when they were able to arrive at a peaceful intensity in the analytic work during a session that this session had lasted much longer than they expected. In other words, after a good session there seemed to have been plenty of time, in contrast to sessions in which nothing much was done and only a superficial relationship existed between the patient and the analyst. Thus timelessness seems to be connected with a very early relationship in which there was perhaps no awareness of the beginning or end of a satisfaction or of the time between satisfactions.

Finally, I would like to return to patient B, who dealt with the passage of time as if it did not exist. In her analysis she related minute and rather boring details of her day-to-day affairs and behaved as if the time available for analytic work were endless. She showed no anxiety at all about not having enough time, since it was up to the analyst to provide it. With these patients I have found that it is usually I who eventually become anxious in case I shall have no time to make any useful contribution to the session.

With all these patients the necessity to grow up is a factor which has a great influence on their ocnophilic and philobatic attitudes. There seems always to be a conflict as to whether a person wishes to grow up, to remain the same, or even to regress. In fact, I think that patients show us their ocnophilic-philobatic attitudes most clearly in analysis by the way they behave towards regression; some seem to have a need to regress which they are not frightened to show us, while others wish only to get on and are frightened of any regressive traits in their behaviour. However, these are merely aphoristic remarks, since the topic needs fuller discussion.

To round off, both the ocnophil and the philobat, in fact all mankind, aim at—and are afraid of—the same ultimate satisfaction, the restoration of the harmonious mix-up with their environment. While the ocnophil gets stuck in the difficulty caused by the spatial and temporal interval between one satisfaction and another, and tries to overcome the distances by clinging to, and magically introjecting, his objects, the philobat is able to detach parts—even large parts—of his libido from the direct satisfaction by his objects and displace them on to the distances in space and time on the one hand, and on his developing skills on the other. The ocnophil *avoids* the distances between objects and satisfactions and tries to *deny* their existence; the philobat transfers parts of his libido from *direct satisfaction* to a skilful overcoming of *the unsatisfactory spaces and times between satisfactions.*

PART IV

CONCLUSIONS

CONCLUSIONS

AFTER having taken my readers on a long and devious journey, I think the point has been reached at which to permit, even to encourage, them to ask: What is the use of all this? It has involved us in coining—and still worse learning—new terms, following lengthy discussions and complicated arguments, re-examining and re-evaluating familiar observations and ways of thinking and feeling. What have we gained by it all? Will our patients have a better chance of recovery? True, what I propose may be a new theory, but have we not theories enough already?

Let me take this last challenge first. We indeed have a good many theories, a number of them relating to the sphere discussed in this book. Perhaps the oldest of them is Jung's about his two types,[1] extravert and introvert, soon followed by Kretschmer,[2] who described the schizoid and the cycloid personalities. These two authors offer descriptive rather than dynamic classifications, useful while discussing people but not really helpful when trying to treat them. Much the same may be said of Freud's attempt at defining three libidinal types: the erotic, the narcissistic, and the obsessional[3]; in fact, this classification has hardly any bearing on our field. More important for our topic is a much earlier attempt by Freud at differentiating two types, the anaclitic and the narcissistic,[4] which in many respects overlap with the two described in this book. Similarly there are many points of agreement between my two types and the two described by Fenichel[5]: the phobic and the counter-phobic.

---

[1] C. G. Jung, *Psychological Types* (German original in 1921), in which many interesting references to older typologies may be found.

[2] Ernst Kretschmer, *Physique and Character* (German original in 1921).

[3] S. Freud, 'Libidinal Types' (German original in 1931), *Collected Papers*, Vol. V.   [4] S. Freud, 'On Narcissism' (1914), *Collected Papers*, Vol. IV.

[5] O. Fenichel, 'The Counter-Phobic Attitude', *Int. J. Psycho-Anal.* (1939).

CONCLUSIONS

Moreover, similarities may easily be established between the well-known anal retaining and preserving attitude and ocnophilia on the one hand, and the phallic-exhibitionistic attitude and philobatism on the other. To some extent these similarities have been discussed in previous chapters; in my opinion they represent secondary re-cathexes of earlier attitudes, and ought to be evaluated as such when interpreting these phenomena during analytic treatment.

On the whole, this might be the chief value of my contribution. It adds—I hope—something interesting to the important field of primitive attitudes towards the world, constituting one more instance of over-determination. Starting with the pre-anaclitic world of the harmonious mix-up, in which as yet there are no objects, my ideas try to describe in some detail the consequences of the emergence of objects. Some people react to this discovery by developing exaggerated object-cathexes, efficient faculties for preserving their important objects and for clinging to them, while neglecting to develop their independent ego; these are the ocnophils. Others react to the same discovery by developing exaggerated ego-cathexes leading to an undue preoccupation with the functions of their ego, the personal skills, and neglecting the development of proper, intimate, and lasting object-relationships. Once again I wish to stress that for the sake of simplicity only the extreme types are discussed.

To turn now to pathology, one may say that ocnophilia is related to self-effacement, to anxiety-proneness, especially in the form of agoraphobia; whereas philobatism may lead to a self-contained detachment, to paranoid attitudes, and possibly to claustrophobia. Depression may be present—as was to be expected—in both, but each copes with it in his specific way; the ocnophil by accepting part-objects in place of the not available whole-object, the philobat by using his skills to get away from his unreliable objects and at the same time by idealising his available 'equipment'.

There are two more points, I think, that justify my attempt.

CONCLUSIONS

One is that the field studied in this book is a clear instance of primitive attitudes which are not 'oral'. The time has come when analytic thinking must break away from the custom of describing everything primitive as 'oral', otherwise our theory will be stultified. I hope my ideas will have contributed to this liberation. The other point is connected with the first. For more than thirty years I have criticised the habit of describing the various forms of relationships to objects exclusively in terms borrowed from biology, i.e. the study of instincts. Instances are: oral dependence or destructiveness, anal hatred and domineering, genital-phallic love, and so on (remarkably, 'vaginal' is never used for this purpose). Although useful up to a point, these terms are restrictive and stultifying. Ocnophilia and philobatism cannot be pressed into this Procrustean system, neither can the attitude towards the harmonious mix-up of primary love. These are strong arguments for my thesis that the developments of instinctual aims—oral, anal, urethral, genital forms of gratification—and of relationships to objects—primary love, ocnophilia and philobatism, narcissism, active adult love, etc.—are two separate processes, though mutually influencing each other. A good deal of obscurity and confusion in our theory could be cleared up if this simple fact were accepted.

Let us now return to the two case histories quoted in the introduction. Doubtless the attitudes of the two patients towards the objects of their environment were primitive and unrealistic, but they conformed remarkably to my two types. Similar primitive attitudes, though mostly not in such pure culture, are met with not infrequently in our patients and, as experience shows, they are not so easy to influence. As a rule, the more completely the various over-determining factors of a complex primitive attitude are interpreted, the better are the chances of a therapeutic change. This rule proved correct in my experience, too; since I have been using my ideas in my interpretations, their efficiency has increased. In Chapters XI and XII I discussed, to some extent, when and how to use this sort of interpretation; my forthcoming book, *The Three Areas of the Mind*, deals with this technical problem in more detail.

To illustrate the atmosphere created by this kind of inter-pretation, let us go back to our funfairs. They offer, in very primitive forms, conditions approximating the two worlds: the world before the discovery of independent objects, the harmonious mix-up with one's environment, and the world which was brought about by the trauma. On the one hand, in the form of aggressive games—shooting, hitting, throwing, shying—the environment identifies itself with the individual to the extent of not minding being damaged or destroyed by him, and even rewarding him for its own destruction. On the other hand, in the form of philobatic amusements—swings, switchbacks, roundabouts—a repetition of the trauma is offered—true, only to an extent that is bearable by a great number of people either as active participants (those who can ride on the amusement machines) or as passive spectators.

In these primitive conditions we may be aggressive or even destructive; the environment falls in with us. There is no need to be afraid that one might hurt or damage anything or that the 'aggressors' might retaliate, might turn into 'perse-cutors'; in fact, we are asked to adopt the role of a ruthless aggressor. The amusement machines, on the other hand, offer us the possibility of repeating in adult life and in bear-able quantities the great traumatic experience of losing our balance, being dropped by our objects, getting perplexed in our orientation in the world, etc. As mentioned, these trau-mas are carefully kept within reason; in fact, the unremem-bered guardians—the inventors, the licensing authorities, and the various showmen—look after us so carefully that it is quite certain that after the mitigated repetition of the trauma—the thrill—we shall be able to regain security.

In this way these primitive amusements provide us with two important experiences. One is being able to abreact a fraction of the original great trauma under safe and tolerable conditions, and the other acquiring a skill which will then enable us to enjoy ourselves a bit more. These new skills, just like the fraction of the trauma which may be abreacted, make us feel up to the mark, capable of dealing with some of our anxieties and thus of restoring—by our own skilled efforts—part of the secure harmony of the friendly mix-up.

In both situations—aggressive games against a permissive environment and the giddy amusement machines—some people feel uneasy or frightened, the freedom is too much for them—or perhaps too little. They cannot face the opportunity offered or, if they summon up enough courage, they feel and behave in an insecure and clumsy fashion; they are inefficient and inhibited in the aggressive games, or are unable to face even that little fraction of the original trauma evoked by a ride on the various machines. Moreover, it does not make any difference to their emotional attitude that they realise intellectually that everything has been devised most carefully and there is no real danger to anybody or anything. As a consequence, they have difficulty in acquiring the minimal skills needed to enjoy the 'thrill' offered. For them—the ocnophils—fear blocks the way of what may be called 'progression for the sake of regression'.

The other type, the philobat, has been able to acquire sufficient skills to ride on all the machines, to participate in the destructive games; he has achieved 'progression' but lost his ability to create and maintain intimate relationships with people. His enjoyment is obvious and open, and this hides the price he had to pay for it. Whereas the ocnophil's inhibitions are public, the philobat's are mostly private, often he is completely unaware of them.

May I repeat for the last time that exactly the same holds true for people's attitude towards their objects of love and hate, towards their original or introjected ideas, beliefs, sentiments, and ideals. To change an irrational and thwarted attitude which mars or foils the patient's relationships is one of the tasks of analytic treatment. In my opinion the most promising way to help the patient achieve this change is to offer him opportunities in the analytic situation for exposing himself to a calculated fraction of the trauma which caused the thwarted attitude so that he may be able to acquire the amount of personal skill needed for the enjoyment of what adult life may bring him; however, all the time a careful watch must be kept that the patient should at the same time retain—or regain—an ability to establish and maintain intimate, and durable, contact with people. In my forthcoming book I intend to discuss in some detail the theoretical and technical problems involved in this kind of psycho-analytic work.

INDEX

INDEX

INDEX

INDEX

INDEX

INDEX